SURVIVING ARROGANCE

How a Patient Saved the Soul of a Surgeon

∽∾∾∽

S. David Nathanson MD

DORRANCE
PUBLISHING CO
EST. 1920
PITTSBURGH, PENNSYLVANIA 15238

Dorrance Publishing Co
585 Alpha Drive
Pittsburgh, PA 15238
Visit our website at *www.dorrancebookstore.com*

ISBN: 978-1-6461-0796-4
eISBN: 978-1-6461-0704-9

CONTENTS

꧁꧂

ACKNOWLEDGMENTS

This memoir was born in my memory of Marianne, a patient who never knew just how much she influenced my life. She enabled me to become conscious of my arrogance. All my patients have been important to me over a long career as a clinical scientist. Some are mentioned in the book. Others have influenced me, but their stories will need to remain secret.

I have spent most of my career at Henry Ford Health System in South-East Michigan and my practice here has flourished and my skills advanced because of many colleagues – doctors, nurses, administrators, medical assistants, surgical trainees, medical students, laboratory technicians, and many others.

My visit to the Esalen Institute in Central California, and my experience there in 1990, created the conditions for my rising consciousness and self-awareness, a state of mind that allowed me to escape my arrogant egotism and become more human again.

All my teachers, from kindergarten, through elementary school, high school, medical school and post-graduate studies enabled me to recognize my reality when I finally found it.

The process of writing a non-fiction piece is not easy for someone used to writing scientific articles. I was lucky enough to attend Julie Silver's writing course for medical professionals at Harvard Medical School where I became aware of the relatively new specialty of Narrative Medicine and learned that many colleagues also felt the urge to write creatively. I embedded myself in books, articles and magazines that address the writing spirit and I was entranced by the creativity of writers. I learned how to communicate my experiences.

I'm so grateful to Brother David Steindl-Rast, an elegant, thoughtful, saintly Benedictine monk, now living in a monastery outside Salzburg, Austria, whose poetic soul, deep intellect and simple appreciation of his fellow man enabled me to recognize that one cannot be cocky and egotistical if one is grateful.

Francis Lu, MD, taught me how to look at movies in a more thoughtful way and to interpret my own spiritual transformation through thorough contemplation and attention to detail.

Susan Leitman, PhD, gave me important ideas as the manuscript evolved and helped me see aspects of each chapter that I would otherwise have missed.

My family helped in many ways, from politely reading the manuscript, to providing me food for thought.

Perdita Finn and Barbara Graham helped edit the manuscript. Mark Matousek helped mold ideas through two writing workshops I attended.

It is a privilege and honor to heal patients and this book is dedicated to all patients everywhere.

INTRODUCTION

❧❧❧

I like to tell stories and the operating room is an almost ideal stage for such theatrical 'performances.'

In Johannesburg, and in many other centers, the operating room was called the 'theater.' The surgeon, like an actor on a stage or in the movies, basically talks throughout the operation, sometimes asking for instruments, teaching young trainees by discussing anatomy, pathology or other pertinent subjects. I like to tell stories during surgical procedures and, because I'm leading the team like the chief pilot in an airplane, everyone in the room is captive to my words. Nobody tells me to stop talking, and they even tell me they love my stories, and that encourages me even more to talk about everything and anything. My stories are now often intended to lighten the tension that sometimes develops in the OR.

In this book, I use personal stories about my experiences with patients, which I believe is useful to 'show' how I started off in my youth as a curious, caring, deep-feeling and emotionally human person, and how I changed during my surgical training in South Africa and the United States. I hope to show that I developed courage, persistence, honor, duty, responsibility and ambition during my training and subsequent surgical oncology practice and how I learned to talk to patients and their families, and to accomplish physical feats that sometimes seemed miraculous. Often my operations resulted in astounding recoveries and, if that happened, I would sometimes be regarded as a superhero.

But, as that superhero, creator of medical miracles, I had a giant ego. Eventually I became something much simpler and yet much more powerful… a humble healer who loves his patients and takes care of their physical and emotional needs. Ultimately it would be one of my patients who would awaken me to the sacredness of every single person, an awakening that empowered a higher consciousness, allowing me to grow, learn, create, invent and share my skills more effectively.

CHAPTER ONE:

༄

A LETHAL TUMOR

Twenty-three-year-old Marianne somehow manages to get up on to the examining table with the help of her mother, sister and me. Her limbs, chest, and head are like small appendages of the huge, easily palpable, and plainly visible abdominal tumor, which is the size of a full-term pregnancy...with quadruplets. Lying there, bewildered, gaunt, and pale, she stares blankly at me over her protuberant belly.

She's like a whale, beached, weak, immobile and struggling to breathe. She looks like she is about to die.

She gazes listlessly at her family, perhaps not even understanding that we're talking about her. The tumor, a paraganglionoma, is malignant and quite rare. It has already spread to the vertebrae in her neck, compressing some of the nerves to her left arm. She takes quite large doses of opioids to control the severe pain. For weeks, she hasn't been able to eat much.

The CT scan shows the enormous tumor that extends from the top of her abdomen, just below the left lung, all the way into her pelvis. It has displaced her left colon, pancreas, kidney and small intestine, moving these organs towards the right side of her abdominal cavity. It abuts the abdominal aorta.

My Wednesday clinic with Don Morton, chief of Surgical Oncology at UCLA is a special treat. I have him to myself seeing new patients all day. I dropped everything when he offered me a fellowship position. A native of South Africa, I did my medical training and first surgical residency in Johannesburg. But I am thrilled to come to California and join the prestigious Surgical Oncology program and experience the high quality of American medical practice first hand.

Dr. Morton is dedicated to both excellent patient care and to research and is pursuing a lifelong dream of curing cancer with immunotherapy. Morton's outpatient clinic is across the street from the main UCLA Medical Center. Twenty clinical surgeons include eleven full time faculty and nine fellows, all of us surgeons at various stages of development and background training, are supported by an ancillary staff of nurses and clinic personnel.

The clinical cases I see are mostly melanomas. Morton has established a referral practice and people come from all over the country, and from some foreign countries, to be treated by a world authority on a disease that is found most commonly in white people of Celtic origin who live in places like Southern California. We also treat cancers that arise in the breast, liver, bone, soft tissues, the pancreas, the gastro-intestinal tract, the adrenal glands, and in other endocrine organs like the thyroid and parathyroid glands in the neck. Morton is licensed to operate on the lungs and we sometimes excise tumors that have metastasized there.

Hollywood is close by and we see many celebrities. I report directly to Doctor Morton but I also work with the other professors. Wednesdays, I spend all day in the clinic with Morton and I see unusual cases referred from all over the world.

We study all of Marianne's pertinent scans, x-rays and notes from her referring physicians. Dressed in an immaculate, starched white coat with his name and title embroidered in blue over the right side of his chest, sporting a crew-cut hairstyle, his Southern drawl vaguely hinting at his rural West Virginia coal-mining origins, he greets Marianne and her mother and sister with a warm smile and kindly blue eyes. They had sought the opinion of one of the pre-eminent surgical oncologists in North America and they're comfortable with his obvious expertise.

He and I discuss her case in his office, the mentor and trainee evaluating a complex and difficult case.

"What should we do with her, David?" he asks.

I try my best to sound erudite on the fly. Wanting to learn about this rare neuro-endocrine malignant tumor, I had studied the standard textbook chapter just prior to accompanying him into the examining room to meet the patient.

I know what most surgeons would say: surgical removal of a massive abdominal tumor that has already spread to other parts of the body should only be done if it causes a specific mechanical problem, such as blocking the intestine, the ureter, or a major blood vessel. It is generally believed that a patient in this condition would have weeks, or perhaps a few months, to live. That's what I say to him. We can't really offer her an operation to save her life.

"What do you think will happen to her if we do nothing?" my chief asks.

"I think she will die."

"Don't you think we should offer her something better? Some hope?"

"Like what?"

He comes up with a most unusual management plan, one that is not in the textbooks. I am quite familiar with his maverick ideas after almost three years working with him, but this one catches me by surprise. He proposes that we start with an operation on her neck to remove the tumor pressing on the nerves to her arm. The next step would be chemotherapy followed by radiation to both the neck and the abdominal tumor and, finally, a highly complex and rarely performed surgical procedure called a "retroperitoneal exenteration," designed to remove the entire tumor and some of the adjacent vital organs, including half the pancreas, the entire spleen, the left kidney, part of the invaded left diaphragm under the lung, and the left part of her colon. I tell him this treatment plan is unprecedented and sounds unrealistic.

"What do you think her chances of living would be if we treated her this way?"

"I don't know for sure. This is such a unique case. Perhaps one percent?"

"Isn't one percent better than zero?"

It seems logical although no-one else in the oncology world uses this kind of reasoning. I shrug my shoulders while slowly nodding my head. After all, he is my boss and he developed an international reputation because he has the courage to try maverick ideas on cases that other oncologists would find hopeless. This case seems hopeless to me.

In talking to Marianne and her family about the plan, I stress the rarity of the tumor, the risks associated with each of the coordinated steps, and the distinct possibility that she could die from the operation or the chemotherapy.

Her mother asks what would happen if we did nothing. I tell her I think it will get worse and eventually result in death.

"How long?" she asks.

That difficult question again. Numbers and statistics, which are available for more common diseases, do not exist for this rare tumor.

"I'm not sure. It could be weeks or months. I don't think it is likely to be years."

"And if we agree to the treatment plan you outlined for her, what will happen?"

"Well, she's young so everything could work out well. Or she might develop serious complications. All operations can potentially result in excessive bleeding or infections. The long and intricate abdominal operation could also be complicated by vital organ failure. It is not uncommon for someone as weak as your daughter to have difficulty breathing which would require prolonged artificial respiration – being aided by a machine that will help her breathe. Organs such as the kidneys can fail and require drugs and machines to take over for a while until her remaining kidney is able to function again. She may develop a serious infection which might be lethal. If she survives a serious infection she could be left with permanent damage to many of her internal organs. If we don't remove the entire tumor, it will grow back where it started, and then she may not live any longer than without any treatment."

I leave the patient and her mother and sister to talk about the options. When I return, Marianne's father is also in the room. They have all decided that the proposed treatment plan is worth trying.

The first step, the removal of the neck metastasis, is done by the neurosurgery team. The medical oncologists take over and give her chemotherapy. She loses all the hair on her head. She is frail, bald, uncomfortable, in pain, eating very little, depressed and curled up in a fetal position in bed. She needs help getting out of bed and walks with difficulty. Now she gets radiation to the abdomen and the neck. Could anything be worse for her?

Her big abdominal operation follows three weeks after completion of the radiation. Like a soldier preparing to charge at dawn into "no man's land," I spend the night before Marianne's surgery repeatedly rehearsing every step of the operation. I imagine and anticipate every contingency, planning how to fix each problem as it arises, and in whatever sequence. I brush up on the anatomy.

I fall asleep with the light on and the textbook open, waking frequently during the night, dreaming nightmarish scenes of internal organs and blood pumping out of large blood vessels, seeing myself rapidly grabbing for the correct instruments, barking orders at OR personnel, jaw clenched and determined to flex every available muscle in the right sequence, preparing for the challenge like a pedigreed stallion at the starting gate at the Belmont.

It is still dark when I leave my house to drive a short distance to the hospital.

Chapter Two:

❧

Learning Surgery

The sounds of the hospital resonate with the rhythm of my leather shoes as I walk briskly along the brown linoleum floor of the Pretoria General Hospital on my first day as a surgical intern. The sounds, smells and sights of the hospital mingle with my urgency to get to ward rounds on time as I head towards the floor to which I've been assigned.

A low buzzing of people talking blends with the urgent stern staccato of doctors' giving orders, patients moaning in pain, young nurses giggling, unoiled gurney wheels squeaking, babies screaming, the sounds of rush hour street traffic permeating through the windows and doors, the joyful summer bird songs and the excited declarations of trainees who, like me, are starting their careers.

The unique and familiar scent of the hospital wards includes a contrasting mixture of the pungent odor of gangrenous limbs, the perfumed fragrance of Jacaranda trees outside the front entrance, the faintly sweet smell of escaped Ether from the operating rooms, the antiseptics in wounds, formaldehyde wafting from the pathology department, and a stale odor of overcooked bacon, breakfast sausage and scrambled eggs standing around in warming ovens ready to feed the patients since three o'clock.

The sun is barely above the horizon. Six forty-five. I dare not be late for the chief registrar's morning rounds. Everyone would know if I arrive late. People would gossip about me over cafeteria meals. I had seen this before as a medical student. I wouldn't want to be the subject of nasty, cynical, wicked stories.

The chief surgeon is there at seven precisely. Some even joke that one can tell the time by his arrival. The second hand has barely passed the twelve when he, in his freshly shined black shoes, enters the hospital ward. He glares briefly at me, the rooky, and, without even a welcoming gesture, turns towards the patients in their beds. A God-like figure, white coat impeccably clean, not a single stain, he walks rapidly from bed to bed, square jaw clenched with determination as the nurses look adoringly at his invincible frame. He stops briefly at the bedside of an elderly patient still groggy from the general anesthetic. The chief looks at him carefully, cautiously lifting the surgical dressing to inspect the wound, a perfectly straight fresh scar, twenty silk sutures impeccably spaced at one-centimeter intervals, healing well. He nods at the patient, and his face remains stern and controlled. Another triumph of modern surgery. He is the reason I chose this profession. I want to be just like him.

Paying attention to every word, I must not miss a single gem. Whatever he says is the absolute truth. A kind of a gospel of faith. A little like the deep faith of the Russian peasants in a Tolstoy novel. Or the Catholic believers, that participate in the Pope's mass in St Peter's square in Rome. My faith in the surgical chief, while different because it is not a spiritual belief, will help me weather the daily uncertainties all doctors experience when administering to patients with complex medical problems. I'm following a hero-like figure, expecting that he will guide me while I take care of our patients. He will oversee my efforts and prevent me from making mistakes. He protects the patients from my inexperienced daily efforts at patient care. His task is not to guide me gently. Instead I must be taught the way he was taught: keeping a highly disciplined and militaristic outlook on clinical care. He learned to operate on soldiers in the Second World War and he brings those same regimented wartime routines to the civilian community he now serves. He orders us around like soldiers because that's all he knows, and it works well.

The nurse who supervises the men's ward is starched inside and out. Her expression is not soft and cuddly; her hair sits flawlessly straight under the starched upright white cap that looks almost like it may have been carved from marble. Fingernails cut short may never have known nail polish. Her breasts are housed in a sensible bra, covered by an impeccably ironed white cotton blouse. Her white stockings disappear under her white skirt, the hem exactly four fingers' breadths below her knee and twenty-six inches below that private place between wind and water.

No – I mustn't look there. Somebody might see me looking. I can't have feelings. I know that already. I can't think of her as a woman. She runs the ward like a navy ship, everything in its place, so clean you cannot see any food stains or even a cigarette butt carelessly stubbed out on the floor by a visitor or a medical student. Scrubbed and spotless. Nobody has the guts to even test her stern composure, her fierce loyalty to her patients and to the hospital she has served for twenty-five years. Barely one hundred years after we learned about aseptic surgical practice from Joseph Lister in Glasgow, Scotland, she is a devoted recruit to the concept of surgical cleanliness, the very enemy of any organism that might dare to invade her patients. If she were to carry a poster board it would say: 'keep out!' She glares disdainfully at the small blue dot on my white coat, the remnant of a slight leak from my pen. She doesn't have to say a word to me; I know that I'm in the dog box and that this should never happen again. My white coat should be spotless. The nurses dare not giggle, wear jewelry or make-up, or wear a dress with even the slightest wrinkle.

The eminent man, my chief, stops to teach at every bed side. He teaches by discussing the details of the patient's disease out loud and within earshot of the patient. I wonder how that person must feel hearing his disease discussed in front of everyone. Maybe the patient in the next bed can also hear. My mother would cringe if she heard anyone talking out loud about her intimate medical secrets but there is no way for any patient to object to this practice. Nobody worries about the patients' privacy. We must say it out loud, whatever the 'it' is.

There is only one exception to these clinical discussions in front of patients: the word 'cancer.' Somehow there is a strong belief that no patient should know that they have cancer. It is a word that evokes great fear because it often means death and suffering. But everything else is fine to talk about. I think about the duplicity when we talk about the patient with gangrene of the leg who needs an amputation; his lifespan may be even less than the guy in the next bed who has stomach cancer. We discuss his disease openly, using words like 'gangrene' and 'amputation' and the association with bad heart disease and stroke. But the patient with the stomach cancer is told he has a 'bad ulcer in his stomach.'

I must stop these thoughts. Treat the patient as an object, a disease, nothing more human. I'll be a better doctor if I do that. If I get caught up in feelings I will be inefficient. Do not, under any circumstances, let down my guard. Make sure that I'm the doctor and the patient is the patient. Don't tell him or her about my private life. Don't complain. Don't explain. My surgical chief is always correct. Case closed.

Ward rounds are complete, and I have my notes and orders. First order of business is to write the prescriptions for all the patients assigned to me. Intravenous fluid orders for all the patients; Check. Medications; Check. Lab orders; Check. Radiology orders; Check. Work notes for the patients to be discharged today; Check. Write notes on all the charts; Check. I do them all as rapidly as possible and my handwriting gets worse with each succeeding chart. No time to go back and talk to the patients. No mistakes allowed.

Three hours after starting my training in general surgery I walk into the outpatient clinic to join the chief registrar.

'You're late,' he yells. 'Don't ever keep me waiting again.'

'I had to do all the orders and notes,' I protest.

'I'm not inviting you to give me excuses. There are no excuses. If you can't do the work, there's the door.'

Stuffing my feelings, I pop an antacid in my mouth. My indigestion will pass. When I am reprimanded again I will pop another antacid. I look carefully at the chief registrar and I'm pretty sure I see faint signs of a white powdery substance on the corner of his mouth. That must be from antacids. He must be as stressed as I am. I wonder how many of the surgery staff and trainees use antacids, trying silently to deny that they are stressed.

Impatient to get into the operating room, I want to do all the big cases that I've dreamed about, read about and imagined ever since I spooked my mother by dissecting a rat on her kitchen table while in high school.

But I must wait until the chief says I can do a case with his supervision. All I'm allowed to do is to cut sutures for him and retract tissues apart while he operates.

'That's too long,' he shouts as I cut a suture.

Cringing every time he does this, I try hard to be perfect. My heart skips a beat when I pick up the scissors. I cut again.

'That's too short,' he yells. 'Are you a cretin? When are you going to get it right?'

Devastated by uncertainty, I keep trying harder. Why can't I do it exactly right? Maybe I wasn't meant to be a surgeon. He will never let me do a case if I don't buck up and get it exact.

Months go by. I try hard every day. Some days go by when he doesn't yell at me. I'm at the point where I'm allowed to suture the skin on some patients when the chief has done all the important stuff inside. It feels wonderful to pick up the forceps in my left hand and the needle driver in my right hand. I think I can do it, but my hands shake as I push the needle through the skin.

'What's the matter with you? Just stick the damn needle through the skin, you idiot!' he yells again. 'No, not there! There!'

Resolving what any self-respecting achiever would do, I clench my jaw even harder. My heartburn flares up and I swallow another Rolaids. At the end of the day I play squash with a friend. Needing to outrun him and win, I feel better the harder I hit the ball. While watching a war or a cowboy movie, I'm uplifted by the swagger and ruthlessness of the actors on the screen. Watching rugby matches on the weekends, I yell with delight when the opposing scrum half is tackled hard and lies stunned on the turf. Back in the hospital corridors I strut like John Wayne, jaw and fists clenched, shoulders back, chin held high, chest puffed out, eyes focused and strong. Just like the chief. If I act like him, I'll be fine. It feels great to yell at the nurses, medical students, secretaries, orderlies and janitors, just like my chief does.

Deep inside me there are memories of major challenges that seemed overwhelming. From early childhood, competing to win at table tennis, trying out for soccer, rugby, grass-hockey, tennis, written examinations in mathematics and physics in high school – I triumphed by putting my head down, concentrating, and focusing on the problem. Never giving up.

Having moved from Pretoria fifty miles south to Johannesburg, I'm in the middle of my fourth post-graduate year of training, now part of the Cardio-Thoracic surgery team. This is a 'sexy' clinical rotation for me because I'm the assistant to the Chief of the Unit. In the early 1960s more daring surgery on the heart had begun and I'm here with a team of highly trained doctors, nurses, and operating room staff. The old Florence Nightingale Maternity hospital, a six- floor facility where I was born, has been converted into the academic Cardio-Thoracic Division, equipped with the latest devices that will allow us to do major operations on the heart, lungs, esophagus and mediastinal structures.

The only sound in the operating room is the swishing of the heart/lung machine. The patient's heart is temporarily and deliberately stopped and the blood flows around his body maintained artificially by the machine and the tubes connected to the major blood vessels. I hardly dare to breathe as highly skilled Mayo-clinic-trained Paul Marchand, places the last Tevdek suture in the sterile artificial aortic valve and then moves the needle to the annulus of the patient's native aortic valve, exposed through an opening in the ascending aorta. This is the last of fourteen sutures, placed with the utmost precision, while I hold the Ross metal retractors that keep the area open. The original valve, beautiful and perfect at birth, developed by an intricate and deliberate sequence of delicate processes starting within weeks of the onset of pregnancy, guided by millions of years of evolutionary pressures during embryological development, functioning well for forty five years before it started to fail, was excised thirty minutes ago because its automatic perfection, partially destroyed by an autoimmune inflammatory response to a streptococcal infection, is no longer good enough to keep the patient alive. A new artificial valve will restore the efficiency of his heart and save his life.

The critical last suture, the one placed deepest in the annulus, is dangerously close to the electrical conduction system of the heart and placing the needle too deep would result in a block of the electrical impulses critical to maintain coordinated contractions of the chambers of the heart. The room is tense because of this and everyone knows that the chief's reputation and the patient's life are highly dependent upon the success of the operation. We all know that, once this suture has been placed, the operation is almost over.

'Hold still,' Dr Marchand commands, even though I haven't moved even a millimeter in at least ten minutes.

The suture is through the endocardial tissue and he pulls the needle through with a delicate movement of his wrist, fingers curled artistically around the needle driver. The tissue is not strong enough to hold the suture and it rips out. It will have to be redone. Now it is almost inevitable that the needle will be placed deeply into the electrical conduction system, assuring the need for a permanent pacemaker, complicating the procedure, prolonging the operation by another hour or more, and making the possibility of complications much higher.

'Goddam idiot!' Marchand yells.

He throws the needle driver on the Mayo table and steps back. The room is even quieter than it had been just fifteen minutes ago. The purring and swishing of the heart/lung machine seems even louder than usual. Nobody looks at him and we dare not look at each other. Without moving, holding the aortic retractors in the same place they had been for the past half hour, I hold my breath. The heart/lung pump technician looks down at the floor, while the circulating nurse freezes in place. The technical assistant keeps both her hands on the Mayo table waiting expectantly for the next command from the chief. The anesthesiologist sits quietly at the head of the table making sure the patient is comfortably and safely unconscious.

The cursing continues as Marchand walks around to my side of the table and kicks me on the shin with the front of his rubber operating room boot.

The pain is intense, and I reflexively bend backward and move my leg, while trying extra hard to keep my hands from moving, which might tear the aortic tissues that I'm holding with my retractors. My mind races while I process the pain and the reason for this violent act, feeling both bewildered and indignant. After pausing briefly, my mind racing and trying to do the right thing, I finally lift the Ross aortic retractors out of the wound, place them carefully on the instrument tray, step back, remove my sterile gloves and gown, turn around and walk out of the operating room, not saying a word and not looking at my chief.

The next day I am summoned to appear before a departmental committee and charged with abandoning a patient and the surgery team at a crucial period during an operation. What I had done was analogous to a soldier leaving his post during a battle with the enemy and nothing I could say exonerated me and my action. The chief's nasty deed, violently attacking me for no apparent reason, which would have landed him in deep trouble in the modern era, is not considered important to explain my response. I am guilty as charged. I am reprimanded, castigated and advised that I would be dismissed if I ever did that again. I am reminded that I am very lucky that they are allowing me to continue my training.

I complete my rotation in cardio-thoracic surgery two months later. Marchand treats me cautiously and with respect during the rest of my time with him. The day before my swansong he calls me into his office and tells me I should consider switching from General Surgery training to cardio-thoracic surgery. I smile politely and tell him that I prefer the path of general surgery.

I'm now a senior registrar in the general surgery unit of Professor D. J. DuPlessis, an internationally renowned surgical giant of Southern Africa. Afternoon rounds in ward twenty-five at the Johannesburg General Hospital. Fifty-two patients upstairs in the women's ward, which looks like a giant church hall, the only privacy provided by flimsy portable curtains on wheels, hardly enough to hide the patient from the prying eyes of all the other patients whose parallel beds are no more than three feet apart from each other in the large space. The intern describes the case to me as the four medical students, two nurses and two other surgical trainees listen and watch.

Ethel, a sixty-six-year-old woman, is recovering four days after we removed half of her pancreas and duodenum for a cancer that had blocked off the common bile duct. It is hardly appropriate to say 'we' since the chief had done the five-hour operation, a difficult procedure that has a thirty-day mortality rate of fifteen percent in the best of hands. The intern and I had kept the area open for DuPlessis, by holding the surrounding organs away with metal retractors. I had cut sutures as the chief applied them to blood vessels and dissected the tissues carefully and methodically, and as he joined the remaining structures in an anatomically appropriate way. The crucial anastomosis was the connection between the pancreatic duct, which normally carries enzymes and fluid into the duodenum to help digest food, and the jejunum, a connection that has a high rate of leaking, a complication that is difficult to diagnose and often leads to death.

The patient seemed to do well the first few days after the surgery, but this afternoon we sense a dramatic change. Her temperature is elevated to one hundred and three degrees Fahrenheit, she is breathing more rapidly, her pulse rate has increased noticeably since we last saw her this morning, and her affect is obtunded, all pointing to the dreaded diagnosis of sepsis, an infection that is likely coming from the operative area deep inside her abdomen, probably from a leak of the pancreatico-jejunal anastomosis.

Management of this complication will be difficult, and the sequence and the choice of treatments are critical. Needing to make sure the chief is involved in the judgments we are about to make to try to save the patient's life, I call him, and he walks over from his office. Walking with fluttering legs to meet the military-inspired chief, whose mere iridescent gaze is enough for me to seek asylum somewhere far away, hoping that he will be more understanding and agreeable, I lead him and the team to the patient's bedside.

A large man with steely blue, unsmiling eyes, Chairman of a large, dynamic and powerful department, a man who cannot tolerate fools and who is known to make grown men cry, looks at her face, feels her pulse, examines her abdomen, and carefully covers her body with a sheet.

He steps back and looks at me, a look that I have known before and which makes me catch my breath.

'You have killed her,' he says icily.

Wincing inwardly, I look at the patient to see whether she heard that statement. Maybe, because she is quite ill and perhaps not completely able to understand everything we say, she has not really comprehended this ghastly accusation.

He walks away from the bed and all of us follow, like rats following the Pied Piper of Hamelin, not knowing what will happen next. We shadow at a respectable distance behind him. All of us, including the nurses, have at some stage experienced his personally derogatory comments. He makes them every day, many times every day and we are not able to respond. Saying something, trying to defend oneself, would make it much worse. He would make more remarks, each one more cutting than the last, until one feels like a Christian exposed to wild beasts in the Roman Forum – innocent, faithful, exposed, defenseless, and doomed.

Stopping outside the door of the ward, glaring ferociously at me, he calmly dictates the plan of action, like a general sending his troops into a battle at dawn. He tolerates no discussion or questions. These are the instructions and they will be carried out precisely as he ordered.

In the days before formal intensive care units, my job is to stay by the patient's side, and to take her blood pressure and pulse every fifteen minutes while monitoring and recording the amount of urine she puts out, making sure that she receives the prescribed antibiotics, other medications and oxygen, and sending off blood tests every six hours. I listen to her lungs and heart with my stethoscope and gently palpate her abdomen every hour, and accompany her to the radiology department for urgent x-rays of her chest and abdomen, monitoring the amount of fluid she receives through her IV and making sure she receives enough electrolytes and fluid to cover the output through her bladder catheter and the unseen losses through breathing and secretions into her gut.

Many hours pass and the only time I leave her side is to go to the bathroom. The ward nurses take pity on me and bring me water, coffee and a sandwich. I am too terrified to request another surgical resident to replace me, reliving the chief's accusations, blaming me for a complication of an operation that he had done.

Sitting like that at her bedside hour after hour is almost like being forced into a meditative trance-like state, reliving how I could have done something different. Perhaps it really is my fault. But how? I had not done the anastomosis that was leaking pancreatic enzymes into the tissues around her pancreas and jejunum and killing her rapidly. We can't expect to save her by doing an emergency operation; that exercise would be futile because the tissues would be too damaged and fragile to be amenable to repair. The rubber drain placed at the time of surgery continues to leak pancreatic enzymes onto the thick dressings. All we can do is support her and hope that her natural reparative processes will heal the leak.

But that is not to be. Over the next day or so she develops all the major complications of sepsis, including failure of the lungs, kidneys, liver, brain and, finally her heart stops.

As the senior resident on the case my torment has only just begun because I must present her death to the entire surgery staff at the dreaded Mortality and Morbidity conference the following Saturday morning.

A new batch of medical students is assigned to me. They're a little apprehensive being filled with book knowledge but very little practical know-how. I strut around the patients, ordering the nurses and orderlies to do things. The medical students will be impressed. I remember what I was like when I was a medical student.

'Nurse, where is this patient? Why isn't he in his bed when I need to examine him?'

'I think he's in the bathroom, doctor,' she says.

'What? You knew I was coming to examine him and you let him go to the bathroom? Are you crazy? I don't have all day! Go and bring him back immediately!'

There you go. Now they will know who's in charge.

I send one of the medical students to get gauze and antiseptic in the dressing room. He walks away, too slowly.

'Hurry up! Move it!'

All the students stop asking me questions. They're scared of my sharp tongue and harsh judgments. That's OK. I can just lecture them. If they're too timid to ask me questions I must be great. I'm doing the job. Education by fear. Just dishing it out the same way that Professor DuPlesis dishes it out to me.

I start my weekend call for all acute surgical emergencies in the Johannesburg General Hospital on Friday morning at dawn. I will be done at seven o'clock on Monday morning. I'm part of the surgical team seeing all one hundred and four inpatients by 8 am. About half a minute per patient contact. It's the hundred-yard dash, not the marathon. No time to linger. The patient needs to ask questions about his disease? His anxious wife, hovering in the corridor, unsure of her husband's fate, looks pleadingly at me as I brush by her on my way to the outpatient clinic. Part of me, deep inside somewhere, wants to stop and talk and empathize with her but I'm in a hurry. She should know that I have important things to do. Too bad. There is no time.

The interns do their part by writing all the orders. I head off to the clinic. One by one the patients enter, and I quickly and thoroughly take an oral history and do a physical examination on each one and make recommendations. In the pre-digital age, I write names and numbers in a book. Planned surgical procedures are scheduled, prescriptions written, and follow-up visits organized. I bark orders at the medical students, nurses and support staff.

After a quick lunch, wolfing down a sandwich and a cup of coffee as quickly as possible, the afternoon clinic continues, and I count myself lucky when, by three o'clock, I haven't yet been called to the emergency room.

I jinxed myself. I shouldn't have thought about the emergency room because the next thing I know the nurse darts into the examining room and announces a call from the emergency department. I need to go down there, stat. There's been a terrible accident and an ambulance brought in a trauma victim.

I drop everything in the clinic and leave the nurse to tell the remaining patients that I have an emergency to attend. No, she can't tell them how long they'll have to wait. They should know by now that this can happen at any time in a public hospital.

The ER physician and I nod at each other. Grim faced he takes me to a cubicle. He pulls aside the curtain. A young woman lies on a gurney, still in her slightly soiled street clothes, stockings and a skirt intact, one high heal still on her foot, the other foot shoeless. She is pale, her skull bashed in, her eyes open, pupils fixed and dilated, not breathing, no heartbeat, and no other outward signs of injury. I listen to her chest with my stethoscope. Silent. I place a small mirror in front of her mouth looking for the faintest sign of condensation. Nothing. It is an hour since she was knocked down by an elderly driver while waiting for a bus. The ambulance arrived as soon as the driver could get there, and she had no vital signs when they rapidly placed her in the ambulance and drove quickly to the ER.

There's no point in trying cardiac resuscitation. She is the only casualty. The ER physician and I look at each other knowingly. We both have done this before. I close her eye lids and cover her with a sheet. Time to complete the paperwork and have the body transferred to forensic pathology.

No time to mourn. No time for me to process this tragic experience. I walk back to the outpatient clinic trying to put the calamity out of my mind. Who was she? What happened to her other shoe? Where was she going? Was she loved? Where do we go after we die?

I can't continue to think about this as I tell my nurse to start sending the patients back into my clinic. I must control myself and be strong. Big boys don't cry.

A patient comes into the examining room complaining of breast pain. What am I supposed to do with that? I start the usual way- what kind of pain? When did it start? Does anything make it worse? Does anything make it better? She talks. A lot. I'm not able to stop her. She wants me to know how unhappy she is with her husband. The kids drive her crazy. They won't listen to her. The next-door neighbor plays his music too loud. I'm not a therapist. I can't help her with those problems. Why am I so irritated? Is it because I can't help her with her breast pain, or is it because I haven't yet processed my feelings about the dead woman in the ER? Or is it because I'm chronically sleep deprived? I need to spend time handling these issues, but I don't have time. I have more patients to see. They need me.

My uneasiness doesn't stop when I do afternoon ward rounds with the other registrars, nurses and medical students. I'm the de facto leader. I'm supposed to know it all. The chief isn't with us. On morning rounds, he leads and decides. Now it's my duty to lead and make the right decisions. I imagine myself the hero of all the characters I aspired to be while growing up and worshipped; the great soldiers, emperors, kings, Olympic champions, sports stars, army warriors, presidents, innovators, teachers, writers and creators. I must never be in doubt. That's what all those other heroes seemed to exemplify. They never questioned their own decisions. I order, and no one questions me.

The intern and I have a quick dinner before running to the operating room to operate on an elderly man with an incarcerated, strangulated groin hernia. We meet the attending physician in the change room. He seems grumpy. We've disturbed a Friday night family dinner. On the telephone he tries to persuade me that we could wait until the next morning to do the surgery. The patient is acutely ill, and his intestine is blocked by the protruding hernia. How can we justify waiting? He would only become much worse overnight. He might die. Dr Gaylis, the on-call attending surgeon, reluctantly agrees to help us.

While operating on the strangulated hernia, the ER calls me urgently. The circulating operating room nurse takes the call and she repeats the words of the ER physician. An elderly man was sitting at the dinner table with his wife when he suddenly complained of severe abdominal and back pain, rose out of his chair and collapsed. He arrived by ambulance and he is only partly conscious. He has a rapid, weak pulse and his systolic blood pressure is sixty millimeters of Mercury. I look at the attending surgeon and he orders me to go down to the ER immediately, while he finishes the hernia case with the intern and a medical student.

My mind races as I run down the stairs. I already know what to expect and everything I learned about a ruptured abdominal aortic aneurysm comes flashing into my mind. I have never seen one before, but I know all the theoretical aspects of the disease. I remember the lecture from medical school days and the chapter on the topic in Schwartz's Surgery textbook. I must do everything super quickly to give him any chance of survival. Even if we manage to get him to the operating room on time the chances of him surviving the operation are slim.

There he is in a cubicle, his wife anxiously holding his hand. He is pale, obese, bald, grimacing in pain, breathing rapidly and barely conscious. We need to get him to the operating room immediately and there are no orderlies around to help wheel him there. No matter. I'm there and I do it with the aid of one of the ER nurses. First, we need an IV in place. It is not so easy to do in a man in shock because his peripheral veins are collapsed. We give him a small dose of morphine for the pain and we're on our way. I've alerted the head nurse in the operating room and she has a staffing problem. She asks me to wait until our other case is complete. I yell at her on the phone. We have minutes to save this guy's life. She had better find somebody to cover the case immediately or we would have a corpse on our hands.

My attending surgeon, who does a lot of vascular surgery in his practice, meets us as we wheel the patient into the operating room. We don't have time for the usual elective antiseptic skin preparation. He calls for the iodine solution and sloshes this all over the patient's abdomen and lower chest while he is still awake. He orders the anesthesiologist to give antibiotics and he places the drapes over the abdomen. We must do a 'crash induction.' Intravenous pentothal and a muscle paralyzing drug, the endotracheal tube is placed, and Dr Gaylis rapidly makes a long incision from the chest to the pubis, and quickly moves organs out of the way, going straight to the back of the abdomen. We were right; a contained rupture of the aorta with massive hemorrhage in the retroperitoneum.

'Aortic clamp,' he demands.

The nurse is ready and hands him the Satinsky clamp. He places this directly above the ruptured aortic aneurysm and clamps the vessel closed. Then he places clamps on the common iliac arteries to limit the amount of blood flowing in the abdominal aorta. We spend a few minutes giving the patient intravenous fluids and a blood transfusion to replace the blood lost into the retroperitoneum. We carefully titrate the volume, so we don't give him too much, painstakingly factoring in the age-related cardiac reserve. He has already had some strain on his heart because he wasn't able to provide enough oxygen to that organ while he was in shock. We also think about the blood going to his kidneys, intestines and other organs and his legs. Time is of the essence. We repair the aorta by replacing it with a Dacron graft and restore the blood flow to vital structures.

At one A.M. the graft is in place and the clamps are removed. Blood flows across our anastomoses and they don't leak. The patient has been on the table for about five hours. We are all relieved to have advanced this far and are looking forward to moving him out into an intensive care bed. Suddenly, as we're closing his abdominal incision, he develops an irregular heart beat and his blood pressure drops. An EKG shows a myocardial event involving a large part of the left ventricle. The arrhythmia starts as premature ventricular contractions and very soon he develops a dangerous ventricular tachycardia.

The anesthesiologist gives him drugs to treat the arrhythmia and makes sure he is getting enough oxygen into his lungs through the endotracheal tube. Nothing works. We stand back as the electric paddles are used to shock his heart. It seems to work for a few seconds but then he develops ventricular fibrillation and his heart stops.

We start external compressions on his chest, a messy business when we're also trying to keep his abdominal incision sterile. A chaotic time as we try every trick to get his heart to start beating again. Please start! How can this be? We stopped the bleeding and spent hours resuscitating him and sewing the graft in place. We almost had him off the table with the blood flowing back into his lower limbs and to his pelvic organs.

An hour of cardiac resuscitation by a skilled team and no heartbeat. Reluctantly my chief 'calls' the case. Everyone steps back. The nurse announces the time of death: 'Two thirty-four.' Another statistic. The chances of surviving a ruptured aortic aneurysm and walking out of the hospital intact is as low as twenty percent in this age group of patients.

It is nineteen hours since I started my weekend on call.

I feel awful. I go over in my mind what we could have done differently to save this man's life. What do we tell his family? I go out to the waiting room with Dr Gaylis and I stand silently as he tells them the bad news. They are stunned. His son-in-law asks how this is possible. How can anyone die in the operating room these days? This is not supposed to happen. Dr Gaylis explains how we did the best we could, and the family still doesn't understand. We're all exhausted, and we offer the family a quiet room to gather their thoughts and mourn. We order in some coffee. There's nothing else we can do. The OR nurses prepare the body for the morgue.

It's my second death for the first of three days on call.

I go back to the front desk of the operating room to retrieve my beeper. There have been seven calls from the ER while we were busy operating. I go down there almost immediately to see all the cases. Two of them need to be admitted to our surgical ward.

One needs an emergency operation.

He is a middle-aged man with severe abdominal pain. He was perfectly fine until just before bedtime when he suddenly had severe pain in his upper abdomen and in both shoulders. An x-ray shows 'free' air under both diaphragms outside of the intestine. He admits to having severe heartburn for a few days partly relieved by chewing antacids. The diagnosis is obvious, and we must take him to the operating room to repair his perforated ulcer. His symptoms of heartburn relieved by antacids are just like mine. I'm convinced I will also get a perforated ulcer.

We start the operation at four thirty. I'm tired and I haven't slept for almost twenty-four hours. But I'm excited to be doing this case. My adrenaline level must be high. I'm running on pure energy. The chief lets me make the incision and explore the upper abdomen while he stands on the opposite side of the table assisting and instructing me. There is a characteristic puffing sound as the air escapes when we open the peritoneal cavity. We find the perforation in the first part of the duodenum and close it with a patch of omentum and close his abdomen. He is otherwise healthy, and he will do well. He will likely go home in a few days on a strict regimen of anti-ulcer therapy and a soft diet.

We're miraculously on time for Saturday morning rounds at six thirty, followed soon after by the Saturday morning mortality and morbidity conference.

The hospital auditorium, filled with surgeons, surgical trainees and medical students, sitting in rows of wooden benches, feels like a court room as I stand at the podium facing them, wearing a clean white shirt, grey flannel trousers, a dark tie, black leather shoes, and a spotless, starched, white coat. The process is meant to be an opportunity to learn from one's mistakes, but it always seems like it is more of a forum for entertaining the audience at my expense. I had agonized for days while preparing for the assault that I expected. I need to anticipate everyone else. Much like a modern presidential debate on television where the candidates will have spent days practicing the answers to anticipated questions, I have studied textbooks and read published papers on the complication I am presenting. I can quote numbers and statistics from all over the world, from the authorities on the topic. How much readier could I be?

All the surgeons are there at M and M, even the ones in private practice in the city. It feels like being in the Circus Maximus during the Roman Empire. I know that it is entertaining for the older surgeons who seem to love watching us young guys squirm and stutter when the chief asks piercing questions in rapid order. When his sharp tongue and quick mind have done their stuff, the other surgeons lay into us with even more questions. The Emperor in Rome would turn his thumb down when the crowd wanted the blood of the gladiator lying on the ground with his victorious opponent standing triumphantly waiting to plunge his sword into the neck of the vanquished one. My fate is similar in a way. Where's my mother when I need her? 'Please, sir, forgive him; he's been up all night taking care of emergencies. He's a good boy, sir. I know he did his best.'

The case presentation is straight forward as I rattle off the patient's demographics, describe how the diagnosis was made, and the details of the operation. I focus intensely on how the anastomosis between the pancreatic duct and the jejunum had been performed. I describe her post-operative course, first identifying the moment we saw her and how we made a diagnosis of sepsis on afternoon rounds, and then how we managed her after that, describing details of the drugs and the intravenous fluids given, and the rapid deterioration until she died.

At first the questions directed at me are designed to clarify some details which I may have missed in my presentation. Then the circus begins as the senior surgeons start analyzing the case pointing out areas where they would have done something completely different. The worst part is when they criticize me for the way I did the anastomosis. I can't say that Professor DuPlessis did the anastomosis. I'm obliged to stand there and 'take it like a man.' Everyone knows that the chief did the anastomosis, but they can't criticize him directly.

The worst part is when DuPlessis ends the discussion by telling me, in front of everyone present, that I need a remedial course in the laboratory on how to do an anastomosis between the pancreatic duct and the jejunum. But, of course, I take it and accept that it was my fault that the complication occurred. Even though I worked with a team of surgeons and ancillary staff and I had not even been the operating surgeon. I just helped the senior guy. But I must not say that. 'Take it on the chin, son, and don't whine.' Once again, I stuff my feelings and swallow another antacid.

23

What is it like to be attacked verbally every day because the fear that one develops was thought at that time to be the best way for a trainee to learn? I always thought it was a British thing, exemplified by the bullying in nineteenth century schools depicted in famous schoolhouse stories such as 'Oliver Twist' by Charles Dickens and in 'Tom Brown's School days' by Thomas Hughes, and many other stories from that era. Modern educators have learned the folly of such beliefs so that most modern surgery training is less likely to expose surgeons in training to fear, relying on a more tender-hearted approach to the process. I experienced the 'tough' way and I did the same to my junior residents.

After M and M, I walk back to the doctors' room outside ward twenty-five to complete the paperwork for all the patient discharges for the week. Professor DuPlessis sits at the head of a large oak table and reads every discharge summary and signs them when they are correct and complete. Often, he finds mistakes and one of the guys must fix it right there. We can't start another week with incomplete and incorrect paperwork from the prior week. Then we review all the lab tests and x-rays for the week. We cannot miss even one abnormal result. We work steadily until mid-afternoon without lunch.

Amazingly I've not been called back to the ER all morning. The inpatients all seem stable and I pray that I can sneak off to the on-call room and sleep for a while. Even an hour would be fine. I have at least that short amount of time before afternoon rounds at 4 pm. I fall fast asleep in minutes, into a deep, desperate sleep but my telephone rings within five minutes of me putting my head on the pillow. It's a sickly feeling waking up like that and even worse when I hear the dreaded words that there is another patient with abdominal pain and a rapid pulse who was dropped off by ambulance. I should get up and get dressed. I walk down the stairs to the ER, even though every fiber in my being is protesting. 'Please, let me sleep. I'll do anything if you let me sleep.'

How can I function when I feel like this? I walk rapidly, trying to clear my mind. My whole being is on automatic pilot as I think through all the conditions that cause abdominal pain and a rapid pulse. I feel exactly like I felt when I drank too much alcohol at a party. I drove home knowing I shouldn't have done that and I was grateful to have arrived home safely when I realized the effect of alcohol on my cognitive functions. My extreme tiredness makes me feel like I drank too much alcohol. I won't ever again drink and drive but there is no law to stop me or to remove me from taking care of patients while I'm in this dangerous sleep-deprived state.

The ER patient has acute hemorrhagic pancreatitis caused by excess alcohol consumption. There's no emergency operation for this disease but we should resuscitate him and stay by his side constantly. This is 1971 and intensive care units have only just recently begun to function. They are crude and under-staffed, and we have only primitive equipment and a relatively poor understanding of the patho-physiology of critical life-threatening diseases. The patient is in shock and we need to pour fluids into his veins, measure his urine output, do blood tests every few hours, take his blood pressure and pulse, and watch his breathing. The monitoring is done by physicians and medical students and I set up a timed schedule around the clock for the team.

It's time for afternoon rounds and we do this with one member of the team absent; he's watching the patient with acute pancreatitis. Two patients already dead and one whose chance of dying is about eighty percent. And I'm exhausted. I can't show my exhaustion. I must be strong. I need to make sure all the inpatients are well taken care of. No mistakes allowed. Be vigilant. Make sure every member of the team is working efficiently.

We finish rounds at six and it is dinner time. I'm not hungry and I don't eat much. I just want to sleep. I'm worried about the patient as I head back to the on-call room. I undress completely and get under the covers. I'm exhausted but my brain won't stop. I toss and turn, mulling over how best to save this patient's life. I turn on the light and open my textbook, looking rapidly through the chapter on pancreatitis. It is long, almost fifty pages, written by a prominent American doctor. Maybe I missed something. Maybe there's a drug I should be giving. I start to drift off to sleep with the book on my chest and the light on.

Suddenly the door to the on-call room opens and in walks the night supervisor, a senior nurse with a flashlight. She is almost as startled as I am as I jump out of bed, completely naked. I grab a pillow to cover myself as she turns pink with embarrassment, turns around, walks out and closes the door. Now I can't decide if I dreamed this strange experience. Why did she come into the doctor's on-call room in the first place? I get back into bed.

The telephone rings and one of the floor nurses is calling to clarify an order. I wrote it precisely, with all my surgical obsessiveness, and now she calls me as I'm trying to sleep? She is pretty and sweet, and I want to keep on her good side, so I don't yell. At least half the calls I receive are probably unnecessary. The nurses must be sure that they have the doctor's orders right. Or, maybe, they really want to flirt. No, not really. That can't be true.

We are all in our twenties and the nurses in training are eighteen, nineteen and twenty years old. They've been thrust into a difficult world of illness, death, suffering, and surgical wounds, and they are bewildered and away from their families and friends, living in the nurses' dormitory. We are a little older and we've had years of medical school to enable us to get used to all this stuff. But am I ever used to it? My childhood friends have no idea about all the human tragedy that I'm exposed to every day. I can't talk to them about it. When I see them at parties I must pretend that the world is as simple and joyful as they think it is.

I try to fall asleep again, but my mind is racing. Images of the dead woman in the ER, the elderly gentleman who died on the table after a five-hour operation, one hundred and four ward patients recovering from various procedures and diseases, the personally derogatory remarks at M and M, and my incessant need to be left alone for a few hours so I can sleep. I'm tense as I anticipate the telephone will ring again. I'm exhausted but I can't sleep.

The loud plumbing noises in the old hospital walls have a familiar rhythm, almost warm and inviting, almost musical. I've heard them before while on call. Not all call nights are the same. Sometimes, when an entire night goes by without a single call, and I relax at the desk in the call room reading my text book, those rhythms are friendly and supportive. But, tonight, they sound like a cacophony, an unpleasant arrangement of intrusive sounds seemingly designed to infiltrate my mind, to irritate me. In the distance, I barely hear the squeaking of food trolleys with poorly oiled wheels, the giggling of young nurses walking down the endless hospital corridors, and an occasional ambulance siren. Interspersed in there I day dream of one of my classmates from high school, at a time when I could kid around and not worry about anyone dying or suffering. I pray for peace, perhaps a happy gathering of friends at a barbecue where I can drink a few beers and forget about all the disasters that modern surgical practice brings.

I try to clear my mind of all the racing memories, ideas and thoughts. Nothing seems to work but I eventually drift off into a disturbed sleep.

My alarm clock wakes me an hour later. It is my turn to monitor the patient with acute pancreatitis. He is stable although I worry about his breathing. We can measure his blood oxygen and carbon dioxide levels, but I must puncture an artery at his wrist to obtain arterial blood. I collect the blood in a special tube, place it in a cardboard box with dry ice and walk it across the street to the South African Institute for Medical Research, the only lab in the entire city of Johannesburg that can run these tests.

The patient shows signs of early respiratory failure. We have crude respirators and no lung medicine experts to help. I make the decision that the patient needs help with his breathing. I place the tube into his trachea myself. No one is expert in the use of the primitive small respirator and I adjust the settings as well as I can. I'll just watch the patient, trying to match his breathing, and re-testing his arterial blood gases to determine the most efficient way to get oxygen into his body and to remove the appropriate amount of carbon dioxide.

The ER calls. I listen to the doctor's description of a patient in end-stage liver failure who is quite yellow and who vomited blood. I don't have to think twice. I've handled a case like this before and I know exactly what to do. The patient has portal hypertension and the veins around his lower esophagus have ruptured and will continue to bleed. I must stop the bleeding with a tube designed by Drs Sengstaken and Blakemore. It has two balloons that need to be inflated in the esophagus and stomach to press on the veins to make them stop bleeding. I find the imported American Football helmet, quite possibly the only one in Johannesburg, in the equipment cupboard. We don't use helmets like this when playing rugby, a ball game like American Football. The mask on the helmet plays a vital role in securing the tube in the correct place. The patient stops bleeding temporarily, giving us time to resuscitate him into the best possible shape to operate. We plan to do a vein bypass operation that will make the dilated veins in his esophagus disappear.

But the patient is still moribund, unable to breathe on his own, and his liver is unable to keep him going. He deteriorates into an irreversible liver coma with kidney and heart failure. Half way through my second consecutive night on call, he is the third patient to die.

I barely have time to organize with our nursing staff the transport of the body to the morgue and try unsuccessfully to contact his family. I have no time to process this death, just like I had no time to process the deaths and rapid-fire problems that I've dealt with since Friday morning. The ER physician doesn't know about these issues when he calls me to see another case at two in the morning.

I'm in automatic mode as I listen to the fair, forty-year-old woman who has pain on the right side of her abdomen. She developed a deep, agonizing pain between her belly button and her breast bone after a lovely dinner at a local restaurant. The pain didn't go away when she took some antacids. She felt slight nauseated. She lay down, hoping that it would ease up over-night. But it seemed to get worse and not better. Her husband drove her to the ER. She has an acute inflammation of her gall bladder caused by gallstones. I'm hoping to get her attack to subside with antibiotics, intravenous fluids and pain-killing medications. If she doesn't get worse over the next six to twelve hours we can avoid an urgent operation and take out her gall bladder in six weeks. I love to operate, and I want as much experience as possible, but I'm so exhausted I don't want to operate today.

It is early Sunday morning, forty-eight hours since I started my call. The patient with the pancreatitis is stable but we watch him carefully. The new patient with cholecystitis is stable and needs to be watched vigilantly to make sure that we operate on her immediately if she shows signs of deteriorating. All one hundred and four patients in wards twenty-four and twenty-five seem to be stable.

The ER is quiet for the moment. Professor DuPlessis is due in at 10 o'clock on Sunday morning for rounds and we need to have everything ready for him. Not a hair out of place, all the wound dressings impeccable, all the surgical trainees and medical students clean, with white shirts, ties, grey flannel pants, black shoes and recently laundered white coats. The patients are part of this important event. They've been told that the chief is coming to make rounds, and that they must be in their beds, with no talking allowed and bed-side radios off.

One hour after the professorial rounds, I head to the cafeteria to get a bite to eat when I'm again summoned to the ER. I have reached a place in my head where the challenge of another case is the external problem. I am not worried about the challenge of taking care of a difficult medical dilemma, but rather the limitations of my own body. I have worked so many hours that I am just too tired to go on. During sleep deprivation, like drunkenness, one of the first things we lose is our self-awareness. This limited way of being encourages a state of mind which pushes us to power on. Until we cannot. I had worked for more than two days, starting at seven o'clock on Friday morning; fifty-four hours with minimal sleep and with erratic bathroom breaks and meals.

'Appendicitis,' is the one word that stands out as I listen to the description from the emergency room physician on the telephone. I don't hear anything else. My ears buzz.

What does a Navy seal do when he is so exhausted that he cannot even raise his arm one more time to pull himself up a wall he is climbing? When it is physically impossible to go on?

My eyes keep closing and I feel irritated, even angry as I walk quickly to the Emergency Department. I can't give up. The patient and my team need me. I use every trick I know to stay awake. After drinking a lot of coffee my hands shake. I replay in my mind some of the words of the Hippocratic Oath that I had recited at my medical school graduation to remind myself that my purpose in life is to take care of sick people who need my help. I think of my nursery school teacher and the important story she told of 'the little engine that could.' Just keep going, I say to myself; I can do it. I feel as though I am running a marathon. I keep my head down and my feet moving. I'm determined to continue.

I quickly confirm the diagnosis of acute appendicitis. He needs an urgent operation to take out the diseased organ. He would almost certainly have died one hundred years ago in the times before antibiotics and safe general anesthesia. Rudolph Valentino, the heart-throb actor in the silent movies, was thirty-one when he died of this disease in 1925. Under different circumstances I would have loved the challenge but all I want to do is sleep. I realize that I am not functioning safely when I call my chief. I tell him how long I've been awake, and that I believe if I operate on the patient it would be unsafe.

'You get to the operating room right now or you'll find yourself without a job,' he says. I know that if I were fired from that position I would have a very hard time finding another surgical training spot anywhere in the country.

Something snaps within me and my response is dangerous because Professor DuPlessis wields such power that no-one can stand up to him. I have reached a point where I don't care what he does or says. I am in a desperate place.

'I'm sorry, sir, but that's not a sensible or safe order and one which the Medical School Dean, the newspapers and radio stations are likely to hear about if the patient dies. So, I'm just going to go home to sleep and you'll just have to find someone else to operate on him.'

I tell the emergency room staff that someone else will see the patient shortly and I walk out to the parking lot.

Driving home is difficult. I should pull off the road on more than one occasion when I start nodding off. But somehow, I manage to stay awake and to get home safely. In a state of exhaustion nothing else matters; I don't need to eat or brush my teeth. I don't even take my work clothes off. I just plop straight on my bed and sleep for fifteen hours.

The next day I go back to work expecting to be yelled at or dismissed from my job, but nothing happens.

Somewhere, deep inside me, I'm grateful that I've survived five years of intense training and I realize that I owe it all to my highly disciplined upbringing.

CHAPTER THREE:

⚬∽⚭

A HEROIC OPERATION

The November sun is just rising above the horizon when I walk into the UCLA hospital at 6.30 A.M. to operate on Marianne. The complex operation seems different from the others I had done before because the type and size of the tumor is so rarely seen. Perhaps only twenty operations like this one would be done every year in Southern California, usually in specialty hospitals like ours. Surgeons, much like Navy Seals or Olympic champions, train rigorously for years to learn the panoply of skills needed to do a "retroperitoneal exenteration," which requires both intense planning beforehand and focused concentration during the procedure. There would be no room for mistakes.

Marianne, bewildered and anxious, covered by stark white sheets on a gurney in the well-lit pre-operative area, looks tiny, overshadowed by her protuberant abdominal mass and the two hovering intravenous fluid bags connected by tubing and plastic cannulas in each of her stick-like arms. A nurse does the checklist "intake" interview and gives her an injection of a mild tranquilizer.

Many people of all kinds scurry by: doctors, nurses, medical students, medical assistants, laboratory technicians, engineers, and janitors with mops. Incessant sounds, like a modern-day, unfinished twelve-tone symphony, envelope the room: beeping sounds of monitoring equipment, ringing telephones, doctors and nurses calling out orders, automatic doors opening and

31

closing, the squeaking of poorly-oiled wheels on mobile equipment and gurneys in the corridors.

Like the intricate and carefully timed interactions between professional musicians playing a Mahler symphony, the timing and sequence of a multipart surgical operation requires a professional and intuitive and well-rehearsed interactions between teams of surgeons, nurses, technicians and anesthesiologists. The scrub technician has all the sterile surgical instruments in the exact order they will be used, and she knows where to find them in seconds. Each instrument is named for the surgeon or hospital where it was first used. The most frequently employed are placed on the "Mayo" table, named after the world-renowned clinic in Rochester, Minnesota. The well-lighted operating room and the interacting teams are ready for a difficult exploration, a journey into an abdomen where even the best pre-operative planning might not be accurate. Unlike a mass-produced automobile, each human body is slightly different from every other and the massive tumor has distorted Marianne's anatomy, occupying space, and creating pressure that has moved organs into unusual places, making for a challenging task. We must react perfectly to unexpected findings.

"Millimeter by millimeter," says Dr Morton.

He and I are a study in contrasts. While he is calm, I am tense. While he is confident, I am unsure. While he is patient, I keep trying to go too fast. I am grateful for his presence as I navigate dangerously close to the abdominal aorta, carefully dissecting the sixteen-pound tumor and the associated organs away from other adjacent vital structures.

Our team's intense attention throughout the entire nine-hour operation assures us that the patient is maintained in the best condition possible. Large blood vessels are tied with sturdy sutures and smaller bleeding vessels are cauterized. The cut ends of the colon are reconnected with Ethicon staples to provide continuity of intestinal function. The pancreas is closed off on its left side with staples and silk sutures. The kidney blood vessels and the ureter are identified and transected between sutures A piece of plastic mesh replaces the partially excised left diaphragm. We carefully lift the enormous tumor and the attached resected organs out through the abdominal incision and hand it to the circulating nurse on its way to the pathology lab.

The last staple has been placed in the abdominal incision. Marianne is unable to breathe on her own and she needs an artificial respirator to breathe for her. Her blood pressure, urine output from her remaining kidney and the blood oxygen—all critical to survival— all look good as we wheel her into the intensive care unit. It is almost five o'clock in the afternoon as I watch through the ICU windows as the sun sets.

Coordinated care by round-the-clock teams of doctors, nurses, pharmacists, physical therapists, dietitians, social workers, and administrative managers is vital since many of Marianne's body functions don't work well enough. Their function will hopefully improve over the next few days. The surgical and ICU teams need to anticipate how much fluid to give; when to give extra electrolytes or blood products to replace losses; when and how to supplement the intravenous diet; how to avoid bedsores; when to change the respirator settings to assure she is getting enough oxygen and getting rid of excess carbon dioxide; when to remove the endotracheal tube, and allow her to breathe on her own; how to prevent pneumonia and blood clots; and how much pain medication to give. Marianne can't talk because of the tube in her mouth while drugs dull her senses.

Four days pass before we finally remove the breathing tube. She can finally breathe on her own. She is very weak and has difficulty eating any food, solid or liquid. She needs intense physical therapy to get her moving. We transfer her to the in-patient floor on the twelfth post-operative day and help her out of bed. She can't stand on her own and eating is a chore. Friends and family – someone – is there all the time encouraging her.

She is discharged home three weeks after the surgery.

Her mother telephones me the next day, and I can sense the distress in her voice.

"I've tried everything, doctor," she says. "I cooked her favorite food, and she took only a mouthful. What can I do? You told me she needs protein to build up her muscles. She won't drink the high-protein drink you recommended. She won't even drink milk."

"Just keep trying. She'll be alright eventually. Everything will get better. It just takes time. Let's see her next week in the clinic and we can discuss this again."

She looks tired and pale, and her wounds are healing well. She struggles to get up on the examining table. She weighs ninety pounds, a scant amount for a woman five feet six inches tall.

Two months pass. I see Marianne regularly in the clinic and try to remain upbeat. Sallow, gaunt, listless and despondent, she needs help to get in and out of her wheelchair and to climb onto the examining table at each visit. She has no interest in seeing friends or family. She spends a lot of time in bed or sitting in a reclining chair, looking out at her mother's garden. Even brushing her teeth is a big effort.

Watching the patient struggle to regain strength is agonizing for her friends and family but I must maintain a sense of hope even while I'm not sure she is going to make it. I guess this is where the hubris of the surgeon may be useful. We survive our rigorous training and develop an arrogance and an ego that allows us to circumnavigate the fear and anxiety we see and sense around us in the family and friends as they watch the patient barely able to get through the day.

But in the deepest of the dark night is the best time to see the stars. Manifestations of hope abound even in the presence of potential disaster: the cherry blossoms in April after a cold winter, the mother parading her ducklings in the spring, a baby's first steps. They exemplify the triumph of the human spirit that chooses hope over despair. So it is when a patient begins to show signs of recovery after months of uncertainty about the outcome. I wasn't completely sure that the massive surgery on our patient would be successful. And to be honest, it's a feeling that still haunts me every time I undertake a complex and dangerous procedure.

But one day, three months after her massive operation, to my relief and astonishment, a smiling, alert Marianne walks into the clinic without help. Her eyes are sparkling, and she is wearing a trace of makeup. Her weight is up five pounds. Her hair has partially grown back so that she is no longer completely bald. She climbs up on the examining bed on her own, and she bubbles with excitement when she tells me she is going back to school.

Her mother smiles triumphantly as if to say: 'We did it!'

As a surgeon, it is always great to save somebody from dying. It makes me feel good to experience Marianne's 'aliveness,' and her renewed passion for living like she had experienced as a young woman before the tumor interrupted her life.

Life is precious and living is something we all tend to take for granted. I have seen many patients recover from cancer surgery but Marianne's recovery, and her new lease on life, seems even more astonishing. Our team had performed a miracle. We had felt immensely respectful of life and reluctant to just let her die, as many doctors, following standard guidelines for treatment, would have done. I am grateful and I remember how I first learned to respect the dead on my first day at medical school.

This makes all our efforts worthwhile.

CHAPTER FOUR:

᠗᠍ᢁᢁᢦ

EXPANDING HEROIC MANLINESS

In 1981, I receive a letter in Sacramento, California where I'm a Chief resident in General Surgery at the UC Davis Medical Center. I am invited to become the Director of Surgical Research at the Henry Ford Hospital in Detroit.

'Are you nuts?' asks my chief on the GI Surgical Service. 'Nobody leaves California to move to Michigan!' Several other surgeons express the same sentiments.

I promptly throw the letter in the garbage.

Three weeks later I receive a telephone call from the HFH Chairman of Surgery's secretary inviting me to have dinner with him at the upcoming American College of Surgeons meeting in San Francisco. I tell her I'm not interested in moving from California to Detroit. She insists that it will be a great dinner. Who am I to argue? On a low salary, a free meal looks good and I am going to be at the meeting anyway.

I meet with Roger Smitth in a four-star restaurant and I have a great meal while Roger talks for an hour. I tell him I don't want to leave California.

'Why don't you come and look?'

I struggle with the idea, think it over for a few days, and I decide to make the trip.

Being from Johannesburg, South Africa, where 'winter' was eight to ten weeks with temperatures in the low 40s at night, and the 60s and sunshine during the day, and no snow or ice, walking in the snow in Detroit for the first time on December 6 is both exciting and unique. It is cold outside but warm and friendly inside. I felt colder in South African Highveld winters inside than I do in the buildings in Detroit because we didn't have indoor heating when I grew up so the temperature in the houses and buildings was just slightly warmer than the outside temperatures. My interviewers even laugh at my jokes. The spacious laboratory is spectacular, and I meet Bernie Fox and Patricia Westrick, the technicians that might be working with me. I slowly realize that the patient population in the Henry Ford Hospital is quite broad, ethnically, culturally and medically diverse, and there would be a great opportunity to grow my intellect and my clinical and research brain.

I must convince my Californian wife to leave her beloved state. I tell her about the great opportunity.

'How long would we be there?'

'I'm guessing two to three years. That will give me enough time to start a research program, write some papers and be ready to move back to California to a University academic position.'

She loves me and she seems OK with that promise. I'm adventurous and willing to try anything. We drive across country from Sacramento in late June 1982 with a four-month old baby in the back seat. Eight days of driving through Nevada, Utah, Wyoming, North Dakota, South Dakota and Illinois, arriving in Michigan in early July.

As a new faculty member of the surgery department at Henry Ford Hospital in Detroit, I attend the Mortality and Morbidity conference on Saturday morning in the Buerki Auditorium. The vascular surgery fellow presents a case. All the surgeons and the residents in training from the different divisions are there. It feels pompous, stiff and rigid, an atmosphere like my experiences at M&Ms in Johannesburg, Los Angeles, Chicago, San Francisco and Sacramento. The discussions are direct and often derogatory towards the residents in training. The senior surgeons relentlessly and repeatedly criticize the trainees at every opportunity, like vultures stripping meat off a carcass and picking at the bones. I listen carefully. I'm the new guy on the block and I'm not a vascular surgeon but I am reading a lot of vascular surgery because I'm preparing to take the American Board of Surgery examination in a few months. I have also done rotations in vascular surgery during my general surgery training in South Africa and in California.

A patient, who had a massive hemorrhage from an aorto-duodenal fistula, is discussed. This is a complication of a prior operation for an abdominal aortic aneurysm, treated by placing a non-biological graft in the space of the aneurysm just below the kidneys. The duodenum, closely related to the top of the mechanical graft, is eroded by the pressure from this foreign material. A hole develops in the third part of the duodenum and leaks enzymes, bile and partly digested food into the space around the hole and this results in an infection that breaks down the anastomosis of the graft to the native aorta. This creates a pathway for blood to leak out of the aorta into the duodenum resulting in massive hemorrhage. This patient had survived long enough to get to the hospital on time where he was rushed immediately to the operating room.

The treatment for this devastating complication is emergency surgery and I had done a few cases like this. The vascular fellow describes the operation and the post-operative course which ended in death of the patient from infection after the surgeons replaced the old graft with a new graft and closed the hole in the duodenum. Some surgeons make a few polite comments while I think the patient might have lived if he'd had a different operation, an operation called an axillo-femoral bypass, an operation I had learned from one of the 'inventors,' William Blaisdell, my surgical chief at UC Davis Medical Center.

I naïvely fail to realize that the operation on this case was done by Emerick Szylagyi, a pioneer of the very aortic aneurysm operation that caused this complication. I raise my hand and confidently comment to the entire auditorium that a different operation might have saved the patient. Dr Szylagyi rises from his seat to defend his team. He is an elegant older gentleman, dressed in a suit and tie, an air of confidence and superiority permeating the space around him. He proceeds to dress me down in a Hungarian accent, to lambast me, asking how I could dare question his efforts, a world authority, while I am a mere young surgical oncologist with minimal experience in this type of surgery, an upstart from California, still inexperienced in my own specialty. I sit there, clenching my jaw, digging my fingernails into the palms of my hand, staring straight ahead at the podium in front of me, holding my breath and breathing only in spurts, and taking the insulting speech in silence while the entire audience listens intently, eager to witness my slaughter, all the while knowing that I'm right.

I leave the auditorium in silence at the completion of the M & M and no one talks to me. In coming days, weeks and months I must show them that I'm tough and that I, too, can criticize the residents and yell at the nurses. I adopt an 'attitude' in keeping with what other attending surgeons exude.

Hovering around the residents taking care of patients, and my laboratory staff, I check everything myself, micromanaging everything, from the medications given, inspection of dressings and wounds, dietary intake, fluid output from every tube and orifice, electrolyte and hemoglobin levels, plans for discharge, and looking for the pathology reports. The residents are a little tense with me because they know I watch every move they make. I pick on them when they tell me something that doesn't fit with my own observations. I become known for my tirades when something goes wrong. Mistakes are not allowed. I'm acting exactly like my surgical teachers who yelled at me at every opportunity. One could never, ever, make a mistake. I'm tough, taught how to be tough from a young age. I had survived bullies.

The sweet easiness of a loving, nurtured childhood ends one day in the Yeoville Boys Elementary School playground during the morning break. I'm carrying my morning winnings, marbles, that I won from other boys, in my pants pockets. I'm pleased with myself. Every time I aim and hit another boy's marble it is mine and I triumphantly take it away and put it in my pocket.

A group of boys watch and corner me near the fence. There are five of them and only one of me. They taunt me and they want my marbles. That's unfair. I won them and they are mine. I tell them to leave me alone. They close in on me and hit me all over. My nose bleeds on my white shirt, striped yellow and blue school tie and my grey flannel pants. They push me to the ground and kick me in the back, tummy, head and chest. I yell for them to stop but they don't. Someone puts his hands into my pockets, takes my marbles, howls delightedly, kicks me again and finally leaves me, a crumpled, bleeding mess on the ground, a whimpering and defeated fourth grade boy.

I get up and, head bowed, walk into the classroom. My classmates look at me quizzically. Mister Lamont comes over.

"What happened to you?" he asks. 'Who did this to you?'

I mumble, begin to tell the story and answer his questions. Yes, I know the boys who did this. They're in another class.

'Stand up and show me how you protected yourself when you were attacked.'

I punch the air as if I were hitting an opponent.

'Is that the best you can do?'

My classmates giggle. What am I supposed to do? Did I do something wrong?

My mother examines my wounds when I get home from school and says it is time for me to learn how to fight. She and my teacher have talked, and she plans to organize for me and a few other boys in the neighborhood to have boxing lessons.

Harry Best is a boxer who teaches young boys around Johannesburg how to box. He comes over on Friday afternoon and we gather curbside and help him take bags of boxing paraphernalia and a large folded carpet out of his black, 1953, Austin sedan and we carry them to our back yard.

We start with exercises. Harry calls them 'calisthenics.' He gives us pep talks. We should build up our muscles and learn how to 'bob and weave,' throw punches, and he shows us how to beat our opponents. We must be quick, smooth and agile. We're going to start with shadow boxing.

'Grab a pair of gloves and stand next to each other in a straight line,' he says. 'Put your left foot forward and bend your arms to protect your face. Make a fist in your gloves. Now I want to see you punch straight with your left hand. Watch me. Ok now with your right hand. Watch me. Ok, good. Now again with your left hand. Keep going. Left, right, left. Good! Now I want to see you bob and weave. Watch me do it and then move your feet and your hips like this. I want to see you move your head and your shoulders. Keep going and do it again. Punch and move your hips and feet. Bob and weave. Pretend there's a bee buzzing around your head trying to sting you. Punch with the left, and then the right. Hit the bee. Good!'

I imagine I'm hitting the boys who hit me in the schoolyard. I move this way and then that way. I'm bobbing and weaving, punching the air in front of me, dancing lightly on my feet. I'm beginning to get it. Hit the other boy and avoid being hit by him. I'm learning to coordinate the movements of my arms, legs, head, shoulders, chest and feet.

Harry dons a large flat glove-like punching bag on his hands and, one by one, we take turns at hitting the target as he moves it around. Up and down, left and right, backwards and forwards and then again, repeating the rapid sequence of movements as we chase after him trying to punch the moving target, all the while staying light on our feet, dancing 'to and fro.'

41

Next is an exercise with a large, heavy punching bag hanging from one of the branches of the loquat tree. We practice punching hard, trying to make the bag move. Left, right, left. My knuckles sting as I hit the heavy bag.

The large, tattered, old carpet, laid out flat on the grass in the middle of the garden, is the boxing ring. Harry chooses partners for each of us. I am paired with Martin Datnow. I don't like him. He lives in a big house, and he thinks he is better than all of us, so I'm eager to try out my new skills on him. He is just as eager to beat me as we go at each other for three rounds. Harry, carrying a stopwatch in his right hand, separates us repeatedly when we get too close and entangled. I feel strong and elated as I land telling blows on his jaw, face and ribs. I'm looking forward to doing this again next Friday afternoon. It is a lot of fun.

I feel more confident every Friday afternoon as the weeks pass by and I get better at bobbing and weaving and landing punches on my opponents. One day during morning break at school I see one of my attackers. He is walking on his own. It is time for revenge. It is the manly thing to do. He is just the first. I plan to attack each one of those kids that stole my marbles. One by one I will find them and beat them up using my new boxing skills. I know their names. This one is Edward and he is walking on the soccer field.

I quickly follow him and quietly gain on him from behind and yell his name. He stops and starts to turn around. I see his eyes, nose, lips and chin and let fly with my right fist, remembering clearly what Harry told me – use the knuckles closest to the thumb, not with the two knuckles closest to the little finger. That way I can protect my hand from breaking a bone. I love the feeling as Edward, taken by surprise, is unable to duck and I hit him with all my might. His nose bleeds and I keep hitting him as he tries to duck and move out of the way and he falls to the ground. Now I'm on top of him, hitting him again and again while he tries to protect his face with his hands. He pleads with me to stop and I remember how he and his friends hit and kicked me when I was on the ground. He tries rolling over and I keep hitting, left, right and left again.

By this time a crowd of boys has gathered and they're egging me on. Finally, one of the teachers comes and pulls me away and sends me to the principal's office. I'm in trouble but I tell the principal how Edward and his friends beat me up a few months ago, how I learned to box and my need to show these bullies that they should not pick on other kids. The principal tells me that is no excuse, that I should have reported the incident to him so that he could take the appropriate action and punish those boys. But I get the feeling that he is quietly supportive of me and he lets me go without punishment.

I'm encouraged and I decide to keep finding my attackers. Two weeks later I spy Richard in the playground and he is not with his buddies. I start towards him but he sees me and starts to run. I chase him up and down the soccer field. He keeps looking over his shoulder as I gain on him. I grab his shirt with my left hand and hit him on the side of the head with my right fist. He turns to face me, adopting a fighting stance. I have my boxing coach in my head and months of boxing practice in my body and I bob and weave and throw punches. He tries to punch back but I'm too quick and I avoid being hit. Then I get him with a combination of a straight left to the ribs, which makes him double over, and then I hit the left side of his face with a right hook, followed by an uppercut to the jaw. He drops to the ground like a stone. One more down, three to go.

Soon I find the other three bullies and, when they're separated from their friends, I quickly beat them up and leave before the teachers can take me back to the principal's office. No one reports me and I'm now the guy that no one dares to bully. Everyone knows not to mess with me, thanks to Harry Best and my Friday afternoon classes.

Bill Lamont is my new fourth grade teacher. He wants me and my class-mates to be little men. None of the women teachers before him ever said any-thing like that. It is great to have a man as my teacher. Lamont takes us outside and we run around the perimeter of the soccer field until we're exhausted. He urges us to do just one more lap and somehow, I find a little extra energy to do it. I want him to notice me and I will do anything to please him.

Anyone who gets less than eighty percent on a test is brought to the front of the class, bent with head over Mr Lamont's table, and he hits your bum with a wooden T-square. I study harder since I never want to be hit on the bum again. The pain is bad but even worse is the humiliation, watched by one's friends.

I learn how to keep strong and fit by exercising, bicycling, shadow boxing, and doing different sports activities. I practice cricket with my brothers, Alan and Michael, in the back yard and with the neighborhood boys and I become a good batsman and leg-spin bowler and am chosen to play in the school team.

I wear a white uniform and put on white protective pads, covering my legs and thighs, thick protective white gloves, ankle-high white boots with studs, and use an oak cricket bat to hit the gleaming red leather ball, aiming for the perimeter, which will give me four runs, or a bigger hit over the perimeter, which will count for six runs. I have a tennis coach, who teaches me how to hit the ball over the net and to time and aim my serve so that my opponent is aced. I'm chosen to play in the school tennis team. In the winter I play soccer, becoming even more aggressive and competitive. I get the feeling that this is what boys are supposed to do on our pathway to becoming strong men.

On the sports field, I learn to compete. I must win every time I enter a competition. 'Practice hard and improve every day' is the motto. Win but be a gentleman. If you lose accept the loss with grace. Come back and fight another day. Keep trying. Never give up.

Bill Lamont is the only male teacher in the school and he gives us projects that the women teachers don't do with their classes. My favorite is making models with Balsa wood. One of these models is a siege or breaching tower, used by soldiers dating back four thousand years to allow an army to scale the walls of a town. He tells us how soldiers and archers climbed up the middle of the tower, constructed on site and how they were protected from projectiles hurled at them from inside the walls. He shows us pictures of the war machines, describes in graphic detail how they were made, invites us to design our own models to scale, and we choose the materials that we'll need. It takes days, sometimes weeks, to accurately measure and cut the wood, glue the pieces together, sandpaper the edges, and stain the structure. Lamont watches and encourages each of us and makes suggestions.

We talk about war in ancient times. The Assyrians, Greeks, Romans and medieval armies. We learn the importance of being strong and manly and to protect our families, possessions, friends and country. We should learn how to read, count, compete and think. I keep repeating the Latin term: 'Mens sana in corpore sane.' A sound mind in a sound body. It makes sense and I'm determined to live that way.

Now we're into modern warfare. The new project is to build a South African Airforce airplane, the fuselage, torpedo-like, symmetrical, painted silver with slots for the carefully sandpapered wings. We read stories about brave soldiers, pilots and navy mariners in the second world war. It is all about heroes and courage and beating the opposing armies.

I supplement my required school reading by reading about other fictional heroes. My favorite is Captain Biggles, who started flying as a teenager in the Royal Flying Corps during the first world war. Initially stressed by the experience he developed into a calm, confident leader. I read every book I can find about him and his team that emerged between the two world wars doing freelance charter piloting in an amphibian aircraft named 'Vandal.' The books are filled with energy, daring, mystery, male bonding with his 'chums,' and very few female characters. He is my hero and I want to be just like him. I'm sure I'll be a pilot when I grow up and I'll fight in wars.

Lamont fills our minds with masculine heroes, both real and imagined. Every day I'm reminded that I must be a real man. I must defend the world from evil.

After school, my friends and I roam free in my backyard and in the large deserted property across the street. We go there despite warnings that bad people hide there and get drunk. They warn us we will be kidnapped and maybe even killed by them and no-one will ever find us. But we are brave and armed with home-made bows and arrows, large wooden sticks and pocket knives.

We look forward to the Saturday matinee cowboy movies. I'm riveted by 'The Searchers,' the first time I see John Wayne in a powerful performance that peppers my dreams for weeks. I feel his manliness. The strong man who saves people and himself is my mantra. I play act the tough cowboy, read comic books about cowboys and learn to be a crack shot with my pellet gun.

My manliness grows as I start my high school days at King Edward VII Boys High School in Houghton, Johannesburg in 1956. The school has impressive buildings, built in the early nineteen hundreds, and improved upon so that we now have a large, new, library; large, well-kept cricket, rugby and athletic fields; an Olympic-size swimming pool; three large dormitories for out-of-town students; and a reputation for academic and sporting excellence. The teachers are all men and I am soon challenged to show masculine courage and strength.

Darby White, the athletic director, has a large belly and a booming Lancashire accent that oozes into my consciousness in the athletic part of my daily education. One day I and twenty-three of my freshman class, dressed in identical black swim suits, line up at the edge of the Olympic size swimming pool at the southeast corner of the large school property. We listen to Darby, the second world war hero, who carried his navigator to safety into Switzerland from the downed plane he had piloted, a feat which won him a Distinguished Flying Cross from the king of England.

'Today we're going to see how brave you are,' he yells. 'See that tall diving board over there? You're going to climb the steps all the way to the top and, one by one, you will dive head first into the pool. You will get the red badge of courage. Those who fail to do this will get the yellow badge of cowardice.'

The diving board is at least thirty feet high and I'm not a good swimmer. I'm scared to dive head first into the water, even from the side of the pool. The other boys in my grade don't look at all concerned and certainly not as scared as I feel. I want the red badge of courage but I don't want to end up paralyzed like a kid I heard about who dove into shallow water and broke his neck. But I don't want to be a coward either. I clench my jaw. What would Captain Biggles do?

We walk in line towards the first step. I'm uneasy and I feel my heart racing. Beads of sweat appear above my lip and just under my nose. How can I get out of this? It feels like a crazy thing to do. I reluctantly follow my friend Ralph up the slippery concrete steps, trying not to look down. My classmates ahead of me keep moving and, one after the other, they reach the top step and dive into the water below. I think I'm going to die. I want to run away. As I pass the fifteen-foot platform time seems to slow to a crawl. Step by step I rise higher and higher and my schoolmates on the deck below look smaller and smaller. Someone behind me whispers that you can break your back if you land flat instead of hands and head first.

As I try to hide my internal panic I think about all the brave cowboys and soldiers who seem to summon courage from somewhere deep inside them when faced with unbelievable odds. I hesitate as I reach the last step and look down at Darby. Just ahead of me Ralph walks slowly but purposefully to the edge of the platform, quickly raising his hands high above his head, bending his head and throwing himself into a dive. I can't see him entering the water but it sounds like a relatively small splash.

I inch to the front of the platform which is covered by black rubber tread and water droplets. Once when I was quite small, my mother had taken me to swim in the Yeoville Public Swimming pool. I remember being scared to get into the water at the shallow end. Someone came up and pushed me into the water at the deep end and I struggled for a few terrifying moments to reach the surface and breathe the air. Without even realizing how to do it I was treading water and keeping my head above the water surface. I felt triumphant as I remembered that event. I can't jump feet first because the drop is so far, I realize I will fall face first. Crawling back down the steps is also kind of crazy and I don't want to wear the yellow badge of cowardice. The only way off is to dive.

I let the platform guide my feet and toes, raise my arms above my head, squeeze my hands together, hold my body tight, and jump forward. The drop seems terrifyingly long as I finally enter the water at a forty-five-degree angle and immediately feel a stinging pain in my chest and tummy. Not quite a belly flop but almost. I'm relieved but I vow I will never do that again.

The boy behind me cannot do it. He stands aside as all the other boys do their dives. I don't remember his name but I do remember Darby screaming at him, calling him a 'dozy dolt,' a term used to describe a stupid person. He makes him come down the diving board steps to the side of the pool and stand there, while all the rest of us stand in line and Darby tells him he's a coward and will be a failure the rest of his life. He praises the rest of us and tells us we have the red badge of courage and we will succeed.

My imaginary heroes are still there and I take out my comic books from their sacred resting place in my cupboard and reread the stories. I need to prove that I'm also a hero. I need to impress my classmates with something even more courageous.

Melvyn and I decide we will do the cross-country race. This is an 'English thing' to do. I had read about it in the novel 'Tom Brown's Schooldays,' by Thomas Hughes. It is about boys at Rugby School in the 1850's who ran a cross country race in the English countryside and it is a story filled with courage, and the hero is a boy, like me, who was able to move out of the misery of being bullied into a place of triumphant strength. The cross-country race described in the story shows a mixture of integrity, courage, logic and a few negative attributes that remind me that the world isn't exactly a nice place all the time.

We start at the school about the middle of the day and the weather is pleasant, a typical Transvaal sky with a few fluffy clouds in the northern suburbs of Johannesburg, and we run through the Houghton suburb, jumping over fences, across shallow streams, fields of long grass, up and down hills, through thick tree-lined forests and back to the school. We realize that we are running against the school's athletic champions so there is no hope of winning. We just want to finish. I imagine I am Tom as I summon up the masculine strength and heroic courage of my literary and movie heroes. At the end I'm tired, hungry, covered in mud and scratches, but happy because I've now shown everyone that I can do a difficult task with dignity and perseverance.

We just walk the final few miles, too exhausted to run, muddied, sore but determined to finish. The sun is setting as we finally cross the finish line. We walk home in silence, too tired to talk. I'm just so happy to have finished the grueling course.

Daily I'm reminded of the heroism of South African soldiers because I walk through the school's main quadrangle between classes. The names of the school alumni who died during the first and second world wars and the Korean war are displayed for everyone to see on the memorial stone cenotaph in the middle of the square. This is a further example of courage and manliness because it highlights the bravery of South African soldiers who fought on the side of the Western allies. This is the site of the annual Armistice Day Memorial, commemorating the ceasefire signed at eleven A.M. on the eleventh day of the eleventh month in 1918 between the allies of world war I and Germany at Compiegne, France, for the cessation of hostilities on the Western front.

Sunday night and another type of ritual. I take out my cadet uniform; leather boots, brass shoulder epaulets, a leather belt, khaki short pants, shirt, school tie, khaki socks, military anklets and leather boots. I spend two hours cleaning, polishing, ironing and hanging everything on a hangar in preparation for cadet drills on Monday morning. Everything must be perfect, boots, belt and epaulets shiny and impeccable, not a crease in the shirt and shorts, and the special hat, like a beret.

I feel special as I ride my bicycle to school on Monday morning feeling the stares of housewives taking their children to school, husbands driving to work, and other kids my age who go to other schools which I'm certain are not as good as mine.

Every Monday morning, I join my platoon for four hours of marching. We all assemble in the large main oak-panel-lined school hall, a place where I'm reminded of the many schoolboys for the past fifty years who sat exactly where I'm sitting. The school mascot is the Teddy Bear, in honor of Teddy Roosevelt, former president of the USA, and it is a rousing memory of a man who was smart, outspoken and tough. We march on the rugby fields, three large grass topped fields that are like hallowed ground. The grounds men keep the grass in impeccable shape and we march up and down. And then up and down again. Left, right, left. Chin up, shoulders back. Arms straight out and in sequence with those legs. Everyone moving their feet in exact lockstep. Then we march out through the school gates onto the roads that encircle the school. Four hours later we are dismissed, and we go to lunch and then afternoon class.

All the boys in the school dress like soldiers on the second Sunday in November. We've been practicing every Monday morning for the entire school year which begins in January in the Southern Hemisphere. For the memorial, in addition to our spotless uniforms and polished accessories, we each carry Lee-Enfield bolt action rifles, also known as 'three-oh-threes.' Carrying the gun makes me feel strong and proud.

Mom finished high school in 1936 and, when the war started in 1939, she volunteered to help nurses and doctors take care of wounded South African soldiers. She told me many stories of the participation of South Africa and its military forces in the North African campaign against the Axis powers of Germany and Italy. The South African 1st and 2nd Infantry Divisions took part in several actions but, on June 21, 1942, after a siege on the town for 241 days, two complete infantry brigades of the 2nd Division were captured at the fall of Tobruk, a major port city in Libya. During the siege numerous injured South African soldiers were shipped back to South Africa and were housed in hospitals and rehabilitation facilities in the major cities, such as Johannesburg, which is where my mother encountered them. She apparently wore a uniform, had a brief training, and helped the nurses and doctors with meals, wound care, and other tasks. This clearly had a major effect on her young mind, so much so that she talked about it to me almost every week for years. The impression she imparted that influenced me the most was of courage, bravery and dignity, three personal attributes that I try to live up to every day.

My father was thirty-two when the second world war broke out, and he told me he was too old to sign up for regular military duties, so he joined a voluntary detachment of men that helped the citizens of Johannesburg with efforts to keep law and order and to protect us from surprise attacks by the Germans. He had a uniform but did not carry a gun. Every house owner had to make sure that heavy curtains and black tape covered all windows and ensured that no light could be seen from the air at night.

Early morning assembly at King Edward VII High School for boys, an exceptionally formal gathering of students and staff in the main hall, a perimeter wall of wood panels on which are inscribed the names of graduates who had achieved a 'first class' in the matriculation examinations going back decades, inspires a feeling of pride and a need to be so honored myself. The hall is quiet with six hundred boys dressed in green blazers with 'KES' emblazoned on the breast pockets, red white and green ties, white shirts, grey flannel trousers, and black shoes, all sitting on old, sturdy wooden chairs, waiting expectantly for the headmaster to enter and approach the podium on the stage.

King Edward VII High School for boys is the best school in the country. The statistics are solid and we're also number two in the whole continent of Africa. We are tops in academics and sports. The stone quadrangle in the center of the building, which was built in 1903, is a testament to the many famous men who graduated here. The cenotaph in the middle of the quadrangle bears inscriptions that show how graduates of the school served in the two World Wars and in the Korean War. St John B. Nitch, an older man, a graduate of a major University in England, hired to be the headmaster of one of the top high schools in Africa, his name conjuring up an image of an old Victorian family, partly bald with some grey hair, academic black robes swaying by his sides, a military stiffness announcing his importance, steely blue eyes scanning the audience, walks in quickly. A strict Englishman, who wears his black academic robes with distinction, he is the headmaster and some of my other teachers are from England or Scotland. Behind him on the stage are seated the senior teachers, some wearing academic robes, representing the departments of mathematics, history, geography, Latin, science, English, Afrikaans, the library, sports and 'home engineering.' His educated voice greets us and we all stand and sing an Anglican hymn, 'All things bright and beautiful.' The headmaster orders us to sit and gathers his papers to give us important information.

One of my classmates turns to his friend on the other side of me and whispers in his ear. Standing near the seated students are the prefects, boys who have already distinguished themselves as leaders and who have the power to punish boys whose behavior is 'out of order.' The prefect assigned to our section hears the whispering and he turns and looks directly at me, eyes ablaze and accusing. After the assembly, he approaches me and gives me a detention. I must stay after school. I protest and tell him I did not whisper to my friend, that it was the boy next to me, but he ignores my plea and tells me I will get a double detention for lying. It is no use protesting so I show up after the last class of the day and find myself in a classroom with two prefects and three other 'delinquents.' I must sit at a desk and write five hundred times: 'I will not talk during assembly.' I clench my teeth and do it while telling myself it is unfair.

Cruel teachers in high school pepper my days. I'm interested in learning but there seems to be a need by some of them to frighten and threaten all the students. This creates an atmosphere in the classroom of resentment, anxiety and fear. My freshman year geography teacher, Bill McCullough, is the worst. We shuffle silently into his classroom after lunch break and quietly take our seats facing the blackboard, not daring to look to the left or to the right, while he stands at the back of the room, dressed in his academic robes, holding his twelve-foot bamboo cane that almost reaches the ceiling, a menacing reminder of his physical threat, an instrument of torture that he uses at the slightest provocation, inflicting pain that is both emotional and somatic. He stands at the back of the room, not in front of us, and he does this deliberately, so we can't see him while he can see every one of us. The lesson is on the blackboard in front of us and we should look straight ahead for all forty-five minutes of the lesson. He reads the words on the blackboard and I write down the notes. In the middle of the lesson I'm not sure of the spelling of a word and I glance quickly to my left at Ralph Dessauer's notes. Immediately after that, within a few seconds, I feel a sharp pain in the back of my head as McCullough's long bamboo cane finds its target, followed by a deep reprimand:

'What do you think you're doing, boy?'

I can't look at him because he is behind me and I'm not allowed to turn around. I don't say a word. The other boys keep still, looking straight ahead.

He yells again: 'Did you hear me?'

'I'm sorry, sir. I couldn't read one of the words on the blackboard, so I looked at Dessauer's notes.'

'You idiot! Don't give me any excuses. Look at the blackboard and listen to what I say!'

I'm trying not to shake. I feel a little queasy and my heart is racing.

McCullough continues in his dry voice as if nothing happened.

It's not as if all my teachers are as mean as McCullough. Most of the others are thoughtful, kind and helpful. Dan Henning helps me a lot when he starts the senior geography lesson at the beginning of the year with an important question.

'I want you to tell the class what you're planning to do after you graduate from high school. We'll start in the front, then go in sequence from front to back in the first row, then from back to front in the second row, then continue like that until we end up in the front on the right. Stand up when you speak to the class.'

I'm in the front on the right and, therefore, the last to speak. I listen as my friends tell the class what they want to do. I have not really decided what I want to do. All I know is that I want to go to university. John Hodgkinson announces he wants to go into medicine. Hillel Hurwitz wants medicine too. My mind is in a whirl of words and ideas, but I know I must say something sensible and decisive and I say: 'Medicine.' The moment I say the word I know that it feels right. I know that I must work hard at getting the grades to get accepted. The medical school in Johannesburg is very difficult to get into and the first year of study starts immediately after high school. There is no intervening undergraduate college degree. I am determined to do it and I know from my experiences in competing that practice, tenacity and hard work will win the day. That's what a real man can do.

My surgical training, first in South Africa, then in North America, with some input from stop-overs in England and Scotland, gave me an enormous ego with a typical surgical personality. In South Africa, where I'm from, surgical trainees were called 'registrars' and 'house officers.' I experienced Professor DJ DuPlessis, the chairman of the surgery department at the University of the Witwatersrand, commonly known as 'Wits,' as a merciless, principled, hard-working surgeon with enormous clinical, surgical, teaching and organizational skills. He did not tolerate fools. He ran a very tight ship, a department populated by high quality surgeons. I missed many family functions, sporting events, movies, weddings, Johannesburg culture and sleep, working at least one hundred hours a week during some of my rotations. My fellow trainees worked like me.

Many of my surgical teachers had worked as surgeons during the second world war and, when they retired from the armed forces, and came to civilian practice, they brought with them the mindset of military medicine. They treated us with the discipline that they used in the army, air force or navy. The hierarchy was heavy with commands, judgements, threats and personally derogatory behavior. I coped as best I could, often by smoking cigarettes, indulging in frenetic sports activities, and raucous, alcohol-infused parties. I could not discuss the emotional stresses I experienced in my surgical training with anyone and I didn't know how to process my stress. I talked to my fellow trainees about our patients but didn't admit to any mistakes that resulted in horrendous complications and death. Instead I 'manned up,' saying nothing about my feelings or emotions, stuffing my caring deep inside, not letting anyone know that I had any problems. I buried my feelings so that I couldn't experience them. Instead I objectified all my patients, thinking only of the triumph of mastering my technical and intellectual talents. Patricia Smith in bed fourteen became known as the 'pancreatitis patient.'

I developed a surgical personality. Surgical training was brutal and proved to be a depersonalizing experience. A mixture of harsh and personally derogatory teachers and lack of sleep made me ruthless. I wanted to be just like my teachers because they seemed unfazed by human pain and suffering. They seemed to walk the hallways of the hospital with their noses in the air, as if they were better than everyone else, and I thought that was the right way to behave. I treated younger trainees under me with the same harshness as I had been treated.

What is a surgical personality? I had learned how to be a surgeon in every sense, often feared by medical students, surgical residents and nurses, using a sharp tongue and an arrogant demeanor to make sure that everything around me functioned like a well-oiled machine. When I walked into the hospital I felt like someone had rolled out the red carpet for me because I was so important. I could take a patient who would otherwise have died of a potentially lethal injury to the operating room and save their life. I could triumphantly inform the family that their loved one would be fine. I was a hero.

CHAPTER FIVE:

ᨓᨓ

ESTABLISHING A CAREER

It takes time to adjust to the Michigan culture and to wear two hats at work – my research hat and my surgical hat. My colleagues in the surgery department think it is a waste of my time to go to my laboratory in the Education & Research building and my basic science colleagues think that I should choose either science or surgery. How can I think that I can be a scientist if I spend half my time in the hospital and clinics? I feel like I'm an alien to both the clinicians and the researchers.

I remove my clinician 'hat' when I'm in my research laboratory but I conduct myself in the lab as a I would in the clinic. I meet the lab staff every morning, as if I were 'making rounds' like I do in the hospital with patients, nurses, residents and medical students.

Lisa, a masters-level lab technician, and Patty, with a degree from the University of Detroit, Mercy, and Pat, with her bachelor's degree and fastidious habits and Bernie, who is doing a PhD in immunology at Wayne State University, think it fun when I start each meeting discussing hypotheses, looking at data from the prior day's experiments, and firmly and decisively plan for the next day, the next week and the next month. I want everything to work perfectly all the time. I discover that every experiment in the lab works well only about one out of every ten experiments and this irritates me because I'm a surgeon and I cannot tolerate mistakes. I watch as Patty injects melanoma tumor cells into syngeneic mice, I oversee her measuring the size of the tumors as they grow in the footpads. I want accurate measurements because they impact the results of the experiment. I work late into the night with Bernie, sitting side by side with him pipetting minute quantities of cells and culture medium into tiny wells in plastic plates, and waiting for hours while the cells incubate at ninety-eight degrees.

Mary, a graduate student in Medical Physics at Oakland University, where I have an adjunct professor appointment, is doing her research studies with me and we are looking at the rates of lymph flow in the legs of mice with and without tumors, and with and without treatment with heat and/or radiation. She and I meet once a week to discuss her experiments.

She is sitting in a chair opposite me at my desk in the office on the fourth floor of the Education and Research Building. We discuss her experiments from the past week and what she found. I look carefully at the data and ask questions. She answers and I ask more questions. She is frustrated and I tell her that she had better get used to this line of questioning because she will have to defend her thesis before a committee one day soon, and she must be prepared to answer many questions, some likely to be more difficult than mine.

Based on the direction of the prior week's experiments, I lay out a plan for the coming week. She shakes her head and tells me what she thinks would be better. We debate back and forth but I'm paying her salary and I want things my way. I'm used to getting my way in the surgery clinics and the operating room.

The frustration grows and she suddenly stands up, hands on her hips, looks at me, shakes her head, turns to her right and walks a few feet, then turns around and walks to the other side of the room, then back to the front of her chair.

'Doctor Nathanson, you may be a great surgeon, you may know a lot about tumor biology, you may know a lot about many things. But when it comes to physics you are functionally illiterate.'

I'm a little taken aback by the brazen insubordination. But I'm used to dealing with unexpected and sudden events. That's what I do all the time in my clinical role.

'Mary, I admit I'm not a physicist. But I am responsible for guiding you in the direction that will convince your graduate committee. I strongly suggest that you do what I tell you to do with the upcoming experiments. If you fail to follow my instructions I will have to inform the university that you are not PhD material.'

Stunned and speechless, she glares at me. Tears well up in her eyes and, silently, she turns around and leaves my office.

I walk south across the bridge connecting my lab in the E & R building to the sixth floor of the clinic building, changing my mindset from lab director to surgical oncologist. The nurses on the eighth floor have done the paperwork on my first clinic patient for the afternoon. That is where I first meet Ralph, a twenty-eight year-old man who works in the hospital blood bank. He had a baseball injury and his shoulder was a problem.

Where I come from hitting a ball with a bat was called 'cricket.' Baseball was a foreign game and we didn't think or talk about it. I'm obliged to learn the baseball jargon. He had 'slid into second' so it was natural that the ER physician who had seen him late one evening thought the uncomfortable swelling of the back of his right shoulder was a hematoma. No bones broken. He had prescribed cold compresses, analgesics, a sling and a prediction that it would disappear 'in a month.' It didn't disappear. Instead it seemed to grow bigger. He is referred to me for further management.

The magnetic resonance image that I order shows a tumor in the right supraspinatus muscle. I do an incision biopsy and it shows a 'peripheral neuro-ectodermal tumor- or PNET.' That is strange because PNET, a small cell tumor like Ewing's sarcoma, is a highly lethal tumor of children, rarely seen in adults.

Les Bricker, my medical oncology colleague and I search the country for experts to gain some insights as to the best treatment, not an easy task in the pre-internet days. But we speak to a pediatric oncologist in Denver who had written papers about anti-neoplastic chemotherapy drugs which Les gives our patient.

After a few months, the systemic chemotherapy is complete. It is time for me to do surgery. Marwan Abouljoud is a chief resident and we work out a procedure not previously performed. We can remove the scapula completely, but this would leave the humerus, the upper arm bone, no longer attached to the shoulder joint and it will likely float upwards, maybe even pressing on the skin of the new shoulder, eventually causing pressure erosion of the skin, or it might 'hang too low,' causing a dragging and pulling that could result in brachial plexus injury in the neck. In prior operations done to prevent this displacement problem after removing the scapula surgeons had used a wrist tendon to secure the humerus, but this technique did not work well because the tendon seemed to lose its strength. We did research in the library and found descriptions by scientists who did experiments in rabbits that proved that synthetic mesh was useful long term in repairing Achilles tendon transection in rabbits. I decided to use that on Ralph.

The operation to remove the scapula, a rarely performed procedure, and one which I had not done before, requires me to study my anatomy textbook. I'm unusually skilled in anatomy having taught gross anatomy to medical, dental, physical therapy and occupational therapy students full-time in Johannesburg for an entire year. I know exactly which muscles, tendons and synovia attach to the scapula, and where the major blood vessels and nerves are in relation to the bone. It is easy for me to imagine how to safely and meticulously remove the entire bone, leaving the right humerus intact with all the related important nerves and blood vessels feeding the arm. I construct a sling of mesh and suture it around the surgical neck of the humerus and around the second rib, creating a crude joint-like mechanical structure.

Time passes. We don't know what to expect. Ralph recovers and goes back to work. I see him regularly in the clinic and then in the corridors next to the blood bank where he works as a supervisor. He functions very well although he doesn't play baseball anymore. When he wears his white coat, you can't tell he doesn't have a scapula. His shoulder contour is almost normal, the humerus still undisplaced. I'm so proud of this achievement that I take every opportunity to tell medical students and other medical personnel what a great outcome I produced. I did something no-one has ever done before and it worked. I write a paper about the operation and it is published in the journal 'Surgery,' a major accomplishment which is bound to make me famous.

I continue to do unusual operations and triumphantly boast about them. Judith's tumor provides me a challenge. Her husband, Jim, is one of the top Ford Motor Company executives when he brings his 44-year-old wife to see me. She has a high-grade sarcoma of the gastrocnemius calf muscle just below the knee, and the advised treatment is an amputation of the leg. But they have heard from one of their friends of a 'limb salvage' approach to soft tissue sarcomas that I am using where I give chemotherapy, followed by radiation, followed by removal of the diseased muscle, leaving the rest of the leg intact.

'I was devastated when they told us I would need an amputation,' she says. 'I play tennis three times a week. I swim regularly. I like to walk in the mountains in Colorado. How am I going to do that with an artificial leg?'

'We're willing to try anything that seems remotely reasonable and sensible,' says Jim. 'Why don't you tell us how it works?'

I admit that the operation is not one widely used and there is no textbook description of how to do it. My background as a lecturer in the anatomy department at my medical school will enable me to design the procedure safely. I also tell them that I have not previously done the operation.

Jim, Judith and their two teenage daughters decide that it is worth trying to save her leg with my unusual protocol.

Fortunately, the clinical management works out well and is completed without a hitch. Six weeks after surgery she discards her walking boot and walks into my office, with a noticeable limp, but a few weeks of physical therapy gives her an almost normal gait. I invite my colleagues to see the triumphant success by asking her to walk up and down the clinic corridor and ask observers to tell me which leg I had operated upon. Nobody can tell the difference and I boast about this at every opportunity I have. I feel tall and strong when I walk around the hospital. People greet me by name. I feel famous.

I continue to grow in stature. I believe in myself and my ability to do anything that is required of me, even when it comes to doing things not previously attempted. Because of my successes, I get referrals from all over the state of Michigan and from neighboring Ohio and Indiana. One of the referrals is from an oncologist in Grand Rapids. Steve Bryant, an Amway Corporation lawyer, has a malignant tumor of the hamstring muscles in his thigh. These types of tumors are very rare, making up about three hundred per year in Michigan, and only a small fraction of those occurring in this site. I have done several operations to remove these hamstring tumors in the past and especially during my surgical oncology fellowship at UCLA.

My initial interaction with Steve is clinical and precise, my usual pattern with all my patients. He is smart and asks a lot of questions. I recommend one dose of chemotherapy, followed by twelve doses of radiation, followed by surgery. He agrees and we arrange to do his surgery three weeks after completion of his radiation.

The operation requires a precise knowledge of the anatomy of the hamstring muscles. I must find and cut the superior attachments to the pelvis, identify the sciatic nerve and preserve it, lift the muscle with the contained tumor off the femur, and transect the distal attachments of the three muscles at the level of the knee, making sure to avoid injuring the arteries and veins and nerves that feed the lower leg. These muscles are important for walking and, particularly extending the leg from the pelvis, and bending the knee. It looks rather drastic to the resident helping me with the surgery and he wonders how the patient will walk.

I love questions like this. I am once more placed in the mode of asking questions designed to be probing and ruthless, using the old-fashioned belief that students learn best when they are stressed.

'Are there other muscles that help bend the knee and extend the thigh.?'

I look at him intensely, seeing only his eyes, a surgical mask covering his face, and says he can't think of any muscles if the main ones are absent. He tries to avoid my direct gaze, looking down at the surgical field.

'Where did you go to medical school? Didn't you learn about the adductor magnus? We are not taking that muscle? I swear you guys these days don't know how to think.'

The operation complete, the patient doing well and a short course of physical therapy follows and, true to form, Steve is walking reasonably well. It also hasn't stopped him from riding one of his three Harley Davidson motorcycles from Grand Rapids to his other home in Phoenix.

He doesn't hesitate to drive his Bentley from his home to downtown Detroit to see me every six months in the clinic, despite the warnings that people in the Motor City might despise foreign cars.

He meets a few surgical residents and medical students during his clinic visits.

'Sir, please walk down the corridor.'

I pick on one of the residents working with me.

'Did you check the patient's chart?'

'Not yet, sir.'

'You've seen him walk. He has no hamstring muscle in one of his thighs. Which one?'

He looks a little awkward.

'I'm sorry but I can't tell any difference between the two sides.'

'Why are you sorry? You're being honest and I asked you the question because I want you to develop your clinical skills and confidence. Let's take him into an examining room.'

I talk to the resident and medical student in front of Steve while he lies prone on the examining table, showing them the long vertical incision from his buttock to the back of the left knee, and then pepper them with questions about the anatomy of the muscles that had been removed, leaving the sciatic nerve covered by a thin layer of skin and subcutaneous tissue. I continue to question them, treating them like I was treated when I was in training, dissecting their answers with more questions. Socrates used this technique with the young people of Athens, never satisfied with answers to questions, always continuing to ask more questions. He was condemned to death for this practice. I remember when I was a young student and how embarrassing it was to have an expert on a subject ask me questions when I only vaguely knew the answers. I believed the teacher felt triumphant when I was stumped with the correct answer. I learned that way, even though it was a difficult and, perhaps, even a painful experience, I am doing the same thing, not realizing that I'm living in a different age and culture, and the students are not happy with my approach.

One year after his surgery Steve asks me when he should stop worrying about a tumor recurrence.

'In general, we have to watch you for life. Most recurrences occur in the first two years. If you get through two years, the chances are much less. If you get to five years without a recurrence the chances would be tiny.'

Every time he sees me he asks the same questions about recurrence.

Five years pass. During that visit, he asks me if he can see my laboratory on the fourth floor of the Education and Research building.

'Of course. As soon as I'm done with my morning clinic I'll take you there.'

Because of his legal background, he is skilled at asking the appropriate questions of me and of my laboratory technicians. He is fascinated with the animal experiments and with studies involving tumor cells seen under a special microscope. He meets Lisa, Patty, Pat and Bernie who do the experiments in my lab.

He is impressed with our laboratory experiments and thanks us for the tour.

The next day the Office of Philanthropy calls me.

'Do you know Mr Steve Bryant?'

'Yes. He's a patient. Why?'

'He dropped off a check for your research.'

'Great.' I imagine a couple of hundred dollars. That was the usual donation from my charity-minded patients. 'How much?' I ask.

'Three hundred and fifty thousand dollars. Do you want us to put it into your Surgical Oncology fund?'

'Yes!'

This news and reward are good for my surgical soul. I am triumphant and I'm quick to talk about it at every opportunity. There is nothing better for the arrogance factor in me than to be able to boast about my triumphs.

This is particularly important because I'm having problems with my chairman. He seems to find fault with a lot of things I do and has said things that make me believe he is about to ask me to leave the institution. He calls me to his office one day.

'Do you remember being called by the senior resident on call at 5 A.M. on Monday morning?'

'Yes. I was on call and a patient came in after a motor vehicle accident with a number of injuries.'

'What time did you see the patient?'

'I think I saw him about 6.45 A.M. I had asked the resident to contact the Orthopedic service to see him urgently.'

'What injuries did you think needed the most urgent attention?'

'He had a compound fracture of the femur.'

'Why didn't you take the patient to the operating room and join the Orthopedic surgeons? You must have known there was a need to internally fix the femur.'

'I was on call from 5 P.M. until 7 A.M. I didn't think it was my role. The Trauma team takes over at 7.'

'Do you know what happened to the patient after the Orthopedic surgeons had completed their internal fixation and closure of the skin wound?'

'No, I don't know. I assumed the Trauma team would take care of him and I had my own patients to see that day.'

'The patient was examined seven hours later, complaining of severe pain and numbness in his leg. He had damage to his femoral artery. It was only then that the Vascular service was consulted. They took the patient to the operating room and repaired his damaged femoral artery and restored blood flow to his leg. You should have recognized that and called the Vascular service early so they could have done the repair at the same time as the internal fixation was done.'

I feel like a cornered rat. The only argument I can think of is that I am not the only one that failed to diagnose the femoral artery damage, a well-known complication of a fractured femur. The orthopedic surgeons did not diagnose that either when they did their operation on him. Nor did the senior attending surgeon from the trauma service who took over from me at 7 A.M.

My chairman is convinced that I'm incompetent, despite six years of surgical service at Henry Ford Hospital, taking night and weekend emergency surgery call four times a month, with no major problems. Despite my pleas he announces his judgment.

'You will no longer take emergency surgery call and I'm cutting your salary accordingly. You will be notified by Human Resources.'

Walking out of his office I look straight ahead as I head for my office. I have a family at home with two little girls who need to be fed and I have expenses that will be at a severe stretch when my already modest salary is decreased. I feel a sense of failure, a deep sense of regret, and my mind races as I try to work out how to survive. The fight or flight reflex kicks in and I immediately feel the manly warrior emerge and, after a few hours, my mind clears and I'm determined I won't voluntarily resign my position. I will stay and see what my chairman does next. The money from Steve will allow me to do research and I have just been informed that my latest NIH grant application has been funded. Besides, my surgical oncology practice is growing. The dermatology department refers all their melanoma patients to me, I'm known for my management of soft tissue sarcomas, like the one that I took out of Steve Bryant, and my breast cancer practice is increasing. I am defiant and determined.

I'm the first surgeon in the department in seventy years of the existence of Henry Ford Hospital to get an NIH R01 grant for research. I'm also the first surgeon to get such a large donation from a grateful patient. I also receive other donations from grateful patients. I'm one of the few physicians at HFH with direct access to a cost center that will allow me to do more research and write more papers. I can do what I'm good at and, if I do that and if I decide I want to go somewhere else to practice and do research, I can.

The internal strong man is intact deep inside me. I'm determined that I will demonstrate that I am competent. I will show everyone that I am one of the top clinicians in the country. To do that I bring out all the resources of my early childhood growth and development, the macho and manly training in high school, and, particularly, the many years of difficult times in my surgical training.

I will prevail.

CHAPTER SIX:

❧

RECONNECTING

Leaving UCLA in 1980 is traumatic. I feel lost and unsure as I head north to join the UC Davis surgery program as a fifth-year resident at the Veterans Administration Hospital in Martinez. I'm required to do two more years of training and I'm fortunate to fill a vacant spot in the highly competitive program directed by renowned trauma and vascular surgeon, William Blaisdell, a friend of Dr Morton.

It is six months since Marianne's surgery and she and her family rely on me to nurse her back to health. She continues to get better and she is visibly shaken when I tell her I'll be leaving in June.

Patients who survive massive surgical procedures rely on their doctor, remembering how close they were to dying. Marianne, so young and now almost fully recovered, is dependent upon me and she is scared that something bad will happen to her when I leave.

'You can visit me if you like. I'll be in Contra Costa County for a year. Not too far from your grandma in Los Altos. You can call me or write to me. I'll always be there for you. Besides, the fellow who is taking over my patients will see you regularly. Dr Morton is there any time you need help.'

She is not totally convinced but somewhat relieved that I'm willing to continue talking to her.

Two months into my new position as chief surgery resident at the VA hospital, Marianne calls to tell me that she is visiting her grandmother, and would like to see me in Pleasant Hill, a sleepy bedroom community five miles from the VA. My wife, who had heard a lot about Marianne, seemed fine with her visiting us on the weekend, even quite excited because she was always eager to take the BART into San Francisco and she and Marianne could go together while I was doing rounds with my patients. They shopped and chatted and seemed to enjoy each other.

I feel a little awkward about having a former patient in my rented house, something my conservative training and medical school dogmas wouldn't approve. But Marianne is so happy to see me that she is quite comfortable. We share stories into the early hours and I open a little bit about my life away from UCLA and my origins in South Africa. She plans to go back to school and to do a graduate program in speech therapy. She is no longer officially my patient, and we warm to each other even more than before. She is anxious to share details about her medical condition since I know so much about her recovery.

She doesn't visit again but we share telephone conversations, letters and cards. Even after leaving California and driving across country to my position in Detroit, we continue to communicate. She graduates from her speech therapy program and lands a job in the Los Angeles School district.

I'm her confidant. She is a twenty-something, living in Southern California, trying to live the life of a typical young woman, falling in love and being devastated when every young man who interests her disappears when he discovers her past tumor history. I listen and console her as much as I can. I find myself using the typical clichés to support her.

'Don't worry. The right guy will come along and he will support you. And you will know it is true love because he will stick around. Believe me, you're lucky those other guys left. They would not have been good for you.'

The frequent communication is great for me since I'm so proud of how I saved her life. Each year that passes reminds me of the ongoing miracle. Whenever I see patients with so-called terminal cancers, I tell her story and how Dr Morton's maverick ideas saved her and other patients like her. I tell my surgical residents to let go of their pessimism when they see cancer patients that seem unlikely to survive. It is quite fine to try something that might work, even if the textbooks don't support the approach, if it doesn't cause harm.

Nine years after her surgery I travel to Southern California to see my brother and Marianne agrees to meet for lunch.

Once a humble neighborhood shopping area, Montana Avenue is as quiet and ordinary as a Midwest town, the homely tranquil neighborhood unchanged from when I left Los Angeles in 1980, is comprised of one- and two-story buildings shaded by leafy trees, block after block of mom-and-pop services for the family neighborhoods. The corner shoe repair shop is still there next to the beauty shop and the dry cleaner is still right next to the restaurant.

Marianne has changed into the beautiful young woman standing in front of me at a bistro in Santa Monica in 1989. Her chemotherapy-induced once bald head is now covered with glorious, long blond hair in a ponytail. Her finely chiseled facial features frame delicate hazel eyes. Her figure fills out a smart pantsuit, very different from the emaciated, frightened, terminally ill twenty-three year-old that I had treated for a rare Stage IV malignant abdominal tumor when I was a fellow in the Surgical Oncology Division at UCLA in 1979. Now she is light, breezy, and comfortable.

We haven't seen each other for a few years after I moved to Michigan. She looks at me intently and smiles as we embrace. I feel like we are close friends rather than doctor and former patient whose chance of survival had been quite slim.

She is so lovely and elegant and she smiles a lot as she relaxes and tells me about her life. We talk about the important highlights that have emerged since our last meeting. She is living like any other thirty-three year-old woman in Southern California in the 1980s, working as a speech therapist in the Los Angeles School district. How different it would have been if she had been treated in the standard way ten years previously, a way of cancer management which had focused heavily on using only supportive therapy for people deemed to be at death's door.

We had taken a big risk with her treatment and here, against all odds, she is not only alive but thriving. When someone is treated with surgery, chemotherapy and radiation therapy, knowing that the chances of surviving even a few weeks are about one percent or less, surviving ten years is miraculous. For her it represents one hundred percent survival. I am so proud of the technological wizardry of modern medicine when I ask her:

'What do you think was the most important part of your successful treatment and recovery?' To my utter surprise and bewilderment, she gives me an almost unbelievable answer.

She doesn't hesitate.

'Esalen.'

I am stunned.

I was expecting her to tell me that my brilliant surgery had saved her life. Hadn't I persisted and supported her when she was home with her mother when she was not able to eat? It wasn't only the nine-hour miracle operation that we did to remove her abdominal tumor. It was everything that happened before, during and after the operation. The decisions at each point in her treatment were so important. Very few surgical teams in that era would have taken her on as a patient, perhaps not even one.

We offered her a course of treatment that I believe saved her life. I had grave doubts that it would work but it did. What better proof is there than seeing her so alive and vivacious here in Santa Monica? What is she telling me? She didn't hesitate for one moment before answering my question. How could she have forgotten the importance of everything we did for her?

Esalen? I'm looking deep into her eyes. Is she kidding me? What nonsense is this?

'What? How can that be? I thought that was a place in Big Sur for pot-smoking, free loving hippies who laze in natural mineral water hot tubs. They didn't remove your tumor. We did. They didn't coordinate the chemotherapy and radiation. We did. I don't understand.'

'Maybe it was a hippie commune in the 1960s but not anymore. Now it's a place for inquisitive seekers to do workshops run by professionals, including psychologists and other types of therapists.'

How could that have been more important than the highest-quality Western medical management at the UCLA Medical Center? What had she done there that made her believe it was so important for her recovery? After all, our team had removed her tumor with a massive, highly disciplined, operation. That's what I thought was important.

Marianne continued. 'I was weak and I thought I was dying after the massive operations on my neck and tummy in November 1979, and the radiation and chemotherapy. One of my friends told me about a weekend workshop on death and dying in Big Sur.'

She had driven to the Esalen Institute on Highway One in Big Sur, about fifty miles north of Hearst Castle, and spent two days doing the workshop. On her way home to Los Angeles, just nine months after her complicated and difficult medical treatment, she was convinced that she was going to live.

I should pay attention. I don't understand how an educated, intelligent woman had spent two days at a weekend workshop on death and dying and how that converted her from a strong belief that she was going to die, even though there was no sign of tumor in her body, to believing that she was going to live.

People had warned me that California was filled with 'fruits and nuts,' that people had alternative views about life that most sensible people in the mid-West did not share. I had lived there and seen a lot of 'free thinking ways,' which I had not experienced in Detroit. In Michigan I had become comfortable with a much more pragmatic approach to life, particularly around the 'Motor City,' where I mixed with automotive engineers, scientists, doctors, and business owners, and particularly with a vast cultural array of hard-working immigrants from Europe and the Middle-East, quite different from the types of people I had mixed with in California.

But, if this dear young lady is so convinced that her healing was from a California retreat, perhaps I need to find out more. I'm looking for something substantial that will help me overcome my confusion.

'What in the workshop made you feel that way?'

'We were encouraged to speak openly about our fears. They listened to my story and they really cared.'

She had met other people with terminal illnesses and spent hours discussing her cancer and listened as others shared their own stories. Fellow patients offered advice about feelings, emotions, yoga, special diets, exercise, vitamins, natural herbs, and the mind/body connection. She realized she was not alone.

Looking back, I now understand that she felt comforted by the milieu of experiential magic and spiritual transformation sometimes experienced at the Esalen Institute, which, at the time of our conversation in 1989, I didn't understand at all. I had spent twenty-two busy years doing surgery and all I knew was the mechanical response to certain diseases, particularly in the field of cancer surgery.

Nothing in her description of Esalen resembled the place that my academic UCLA physician and scientist colleagues had judged so harshly when they had talked in a derogatory manner about the Central California hide-out. I lived in a monistic, materialistic, scientific world and I believed in hypothesis-driven experimental evidence, and had no time for transcendental and non-scientific viewpoints.

I had no time for anyone who believed anything different to what I believed. I was used to dogmatic beliefs in the clinic and in the operating room. Nobody could teach me anything after fifteen years of postgraduate general and specialty surgical and research training and seven years in practice as an attending surgeon in Michigan.

Mine was the very epitome of the 'surgical personality.'

Comforted by her first experience at Esalen, Marianne had attended workshops there every year for eight years while gaining strength, obtaining a master's degree, and working with children.

As I became increasingly curious I listened as she described other workshops and her belief in the feelings that inspired her while there. She loved the tranquility of the gardens and the stars at night while sitting in the hot tubs. She loved the camaraderie of fellow workshop attendees. She felt a spiritual connection with the Esselen Indians who had lived there seven hundred years ago; she believed that the current grounds were sacred burial grounds for the tribe. She enjoyed the food, much of it fresh from the gardens, that made her feel wholesome.

'How do you think those experiences were able to kill tumor cells in your body?'

As soon as I ask that question I want to take it back. I see the hurt expression in her eyes. But she recovers quickly and talks calmly.

'I can see how you might doubt the value of alternative methods of treatment, especially since I know you are so heavily invested in Western Medicine. Don't get me wrong: I know how important you and Dr Morton were to my initial treatment. I know that Esalen could not have done what the UCLA team did. What I've learned is that physicians are so invested in provable science that they forget that there are many valuable additional treatments used by people used to ancient traditions. For me the conversion was easy because I felt so good and I just believe that there is something going on with my immune system that happened only because of Esalen. I believe that feeling good enhances my immune system.'

The lunch over, we hug and part in good spirits but I can't get away from my uneasiness at what I've just heard. I had heard other people expand upon beliefs in alternative medical treatments, and I had not tried to alter those beliefs. I listened and believed the feelings were not based upon science and, therefore, not believable. But I had known Marianne 'inside out,' seen her at her most vulnerable, and I needed to think about my experience with her at the restaurant.

One of the ways for me to expand my newly gained knowledge is to explore Esalen a little more. I call the institute and ask them to send me a catalogue. This should give me an idea of what to do next.

After a little research in the HFH library, and examining the Esalen catalogue, I discover that there are many different types of workshops. I notice the workshops are run by professionals, some from academia, some from private psychology practices, and some dealing with subjects as widely ranging as yoga, music, art, photography, gardening, theology, Eastern philosophies, meditation, and various methods of mind-body practice named after such legendary figures as Rolf and Reich, names that are vaguely familiar, possibly because I like reading widely and may have seen the names before. I'm interested enough that I continue to look through the catalogue, mapping out a strategy for myself if I were ever courageous enough to leave the certainty of my surgical field for a few days and travel to the West coast to give myself a greater insight into what had happened to Marianne.

Days pass and I keep thinking about going to Esalen but, like St Augustine's confession to God, his gathering feeling that he needed to live a celibate life seems a little premature. 'Not quite yet,' is his rationalization. So, I keep thinking I want to do this, to go to Esalen, but not quite yet.

Towards the end of 1989, six months after my lunch with Marianne, while still reeling from my demotion from doing trauma call, and having my salary at the HFH cut by one third, I'm in an emotional turmoil, not clear how to look at my career.

I can plan a trip out West in March of 1990

I felt I needed to experience the Esalen Institute for myself.

I take time off work and book a five-day workshop at the Institute thinking it will be just like many other workshops I attend for educational purposes. My experience at scientific and surgery workshops are predictable if somewhat the same as my experiences at medical school and surgical residency training. I dress in a coat and tie, carry a notebook and pen, listen to presentations, and take notes. That was what I expected for my first workshop at Esalen.

Instead I had an experience that was so profound, so life-enhancing, that it took me years to process and understand. I could not talk about the experience to my physician or scientist friends for twenty years. I even stopped confiding in my family and close friends when I realized that no-one could really understand such an epiphany unless they themselves had experienced something so insightful.

I was to experience a transformation in my conscious understanding of myself and of the universe.

CHAPTER SEVEN:

❦

TRANSFORMATION

I turn off Highway 1 to the Esalen Institute near Big Sur on a foggy March afternoon. My eyes survey a riot of colors and forms: a plateau of gardens, filled with flowers and vegetables, towering trees separated by large fields of mowed lawn, sparse old motel-style wooden buildings, a swimming pool, and the Pacific Ocean about one hundred feet below the steep cliffs. Everything seems quiet, the only sound is the waves crashing on the rocks below.

After a buffet-style dinner in the large communal dining room with long wooden tables, I make my way to the workshop room named for the famous American humanistic psychologist Abraham Maslow. The green-carpeted room for the five-day experiential workshop, "Introduction to Esalen," is furnished with large pillows and four giant loudspeakers mounted in each corner.

Workshop leader Benjie greets the eight participants and we introduce ourselves. Ilene, a nurse from Portland, Oregon, is the only other medically-oriented person there. The others seem to be mature, educated, inquisitive people from New York, Toronto, San Jose, and Southern California.

'Let's stand and walk slowly around the room,' says Benjie. He turns on pulsating, evocative music. We walk around, carefully avoiding each other. No touching. No looking into each other's eyes. It is no different from walking down the sidewalk of any major city or down a busy hospital corridor. We stop when the music stops.

'Great. Now we're going to repeat the exercise. But this time I want you to deliberately bump into each other as often as you can.'

The first time I bump into Robin, she and I smile, while we glance into each other's eyes with joyful surprise and a bit of embarrassment. Then I bump into Connie, a meticulously coiffed county supervisor. Her face beams, while I laugh. Then I bump into Jim, an executive in a large Canadian paper company, which sets off an almost unstoppable bout of giggling. Suddenly we're like little children who feel as if we have known each other forever.

We meet at the hot tubs after lunch the following day. The closer I come to the bottom of the steep, sand pathway to the hot tubs, the closer I am to the waves crashing on the rocky beach below. I look for the men's change room in the grey concrete building just above the beach. To my surprise, instead of separate facilities for men and women to change clothes, they are changing in the same space!

Alright. I can deal with this. I'm used to seeing naked bodies. No big deal.

But I am not used to being naked myself in mixed company. I feel awkward as I take my clothes off. The seven other workshop participants look as uneasy as I feel. Just yesterday we didn't know each other and now we're naked face to face!

Lioness, a woman with long red hair down to her bare waist, greets us and then escorts us to a prepared hot tub with flower petals sprinkled on the water and incense burning along the edges.

'Please get in and hold hands. Today we're going to learn the art of massage. Massage is an ancient art that requires two-way directional communications between the masseuse and the subject. We start by raising our eyes, minds, souls and arms to the universe. We bring the energy of the universe into the bodies of our client.'

Sure. Uh huh. Where did it say this in any of my medical textbooks? Perhaps my friends were right. This place and the people who come here are a bit crazy.

But wait a moment. I came here to discover how it had enlightened Marianne. I owe it to myself and to her to keep an open mind. I scold myself. Stop it! Treat it like an experiment. Try it. See what happens.

After we soak for fifteen minutes in the hot tub holding hands, Lioness invites us to choose a partner and alternate massaging each other.

We climb out of the hot tub and stand by four massage tables, two people for each table.

Connie, uncomfortably tense on the massage table, looks quizzically at me as I stand above her ready to do my first massage. She closes her eyes. Taking in a deep breath, I close my eyes, raise my hands towards the heavens, imagine a vast source of energy, and slowly bring whatever it is down towards her body.

Suddenly I feel a strange resistance in my hands. It doesn't feel at all like the tissues I palpate in patients in my clinical practice. I open my eyes and see my hands close to her abdominal skin. My fingers aren't touching anything. Lioness watches intently and nods.

Impossible! How could I feel a palpable energy field around her body? This cannot be happening to me. I'm a scientist. Well, then, I shouldn't interfere with the experiment. I should observe, be totally objective, non-judgmental, and follow the process to the end. Like any good scientist who has just made a discovery, I should repeat the procedure and see whether I find the same results.

I do it over again. I close my eyes and repeat the steps exactly as I'd done before. I bring my hands down again. Just as before, I feel a distinct resistance about four inches above her abdomen. I look around as Lioness watches my confusion. I have confirmed my original observation and discovered an inexplicable phenomenon entirely new to me.

Something quite strange has just happened to me. I breathe rapidly, and it seems like my whole world has turned upside down. I feel bewildered as my perceptions of reality disintegrate like sandcastles on the beach at high tide. My world of scientific certainty cannot explain this experience. Perhaps there are energy forces out there after all. I had been trained to examine the evidence, and here I have experienced a new reality that I can't explain.

Could Marianne have been correct about what really cured her?

I, along with my seven new experiential workshop friends, explore other techniques with Benjie that are designed to "expand the mind." I had heard their names, but I had no idea of the meaning or use of Gestalt therapy, guided imagery, and other such techniques. I am more used to scientific workshops where surgeons, dressed in suits, sit in auditoriums watching slide presentations, intent on learning the latest medical research, the farthest goal from exploring their own "inner self."

Each experiential session in the Maslow Room enhances my moment-to-moment awareness, which draws me deeper into my own inner world. In contrast to the usual scientific style of talking to colleagues at academic meetings, I begin to express myself during the workshop in ways completely natural and comfortable without inner editing. During a dance session, I whirl like a Dervish, completely uninhibited and deliriously happy.

By the fourth day, I have shed most of my identification as the person I thought I was: the man known by the name on a birth certificate and driver's license; defined by my academic education, my medical degree, my job as a surgeon, the clothes I wear, the house I live in, the car I drive; my job as a clinician/scientist, teacher, funded researcher; my social connections as a husband, friend, son, father, neighbor, sportsman, and foreign medical graduate. None of those attributes seem to matter. I relate instead to my identity as a person living in the present.

Every day I return to the hot tubs to enjoy the freedom of being in the mineral springs and gazing endlessly at the ocean to the West while talking to other people seeking a new truth. Now I undress without embarrassment. Without clothes I am bare and open. I can't hide or pretend. I do not need to be defined by what others think of me. How limiting to be contained and inhibited by the expectations of others! I am just me.

My deepest and most enduring transformation starts on the fourth day with my typical Esalen breakfast: raisins, grated coconuts, boiled prunes, cooked oatmeal cereal topped with honey and bananas, hot chamomile tea with lemon, orange juice, an apple and freshly baked multigrain bread. The rising sun, seen through the misty fog, casts an ethereal light from the East, caressing the gentle waves of the Pacific Ocean below the flat plateau of grass lawns, evergreen trees, and vegetable gardens. A soft breeze drifts across the flowers while Monarch butterflies flutter quietly, gathering nourishment from the milkweeds, thistles, alfalfa, and lilac for their southern journey. Hummingbirds fly their endless calorie-seeking forked tongues from one honeysuckle to the next. Significant by its absence are the modern noises of a busy American city: its intruding and stressful cacophonies, surly pedestrians and health-sapping exhaust fumes. It is the beginning of a new tranquility, barely interrupted by quiet, unobtrusive conversations of workshop attendees.

The Maslow Room, like a warm womb, comforts and protects my soul and my physical body from the stresses of my everyday life. Benjie encourages us to start this morning as he has for the prior three mornings: by sharing thoughts about the last evening workshop session. After a few yoga movements and muscle stretches, we lie parallel to each other on the green carpeted floor facing the ceiling and skylight.

'Close your eyes and breathe deeply and slowly. Follow your breath in your mind. Watch the air entering your lungs, blood vessels, heart, spleen, liver, perineum, toes, and fingers.'

Benjie starts the music softly and, eventually there is an increased momentum as African drum beats and the occasional guttural male voices pulse through my ears. Amazingly, I imagine I am at home in my native South Africa.

'Breathe faster.'

Breathing deeply and rapidly, I think about the physiological effects of hyperventilation. I can't help it even though Benjie told us to clear our minds of extraneous thoughts.

Everything that happens to the human body is an opportunity to observe, to think about what is happening at a biochemical and molecular level. That's how I was trained. I am not surprised as my fingers start to tingle, then my hands, feet and lips. This is calcium in my blood in a different form because of the alkalinity induced by rapid breathing.

'Stop the chatter in your brains,' says Benjie. 'Focus on a part of your body while you continue to breathe rapidly.'

I focus on my toes. They tingle, and then I can't feel them.

Visions appear that are accompanied by a different emotion and sensation for each vision. The first vision, of all things, is Mister Woodruff's ninth grade art class. We are sitting in the garden of Buxton House, one of the dormitories at King Edward VII high school in Johannesburg, near a giant oak tree on a warm summer day, listening to all the distinct sounds in unison: the virtuoso sounds of birds chirping, the chatter of the gardeners as they water flower beds and lawns, the giggling of housemaids talking to each other across the neighboring fences, the sounds of car engines changing gears as they negotiate the steep hill close to the school, the energetic splash of competitive swimmers training in the nearby pool, the low bass voice of the geography teacher wafting out of the open second floor window, and the enigmatic buzzing of insects. All the while I see the fluffy white clouds in a radiant blue Transvaal sky, and I feel the charcoal in my hands draw the tree on a blank piece of art paper.

As the music changes to a Bach fugue I start to rise toward the ceiling.

Wow! What is this? What is happening?

Stop thinking and do not question this, I tell myself. Do not open your eyes. Just go with it.

I keep breathing rapidly as if that is the engine for my flying adventure; to stop would mean I would tumble rapidly to the land below. Even though I don't know where I'm heading, I feel elated. My magic carpet keeps rising, moving faster into the air around the room, through the ceiling, out over the gardens and the ocean, towards the heavens, filled with bright stars, planets, the moon, and the unknown. I try lifting my arms, but they are numb. I fly past echelons of geese in a penetratingly eerie silence. I recognize the images of friends, children, siblings, cousins, teachers, heroes, and historical figures as they whizz by.

I keep moving faster and faster past flashing lights and a brilliant array of colors like the spaceship approaching Jupiter in the movie "*2001: A Space Odyssey.*" I keep breathing fast and deeply.

My visual images shift when the music changes again. Suddenly I hear the rhythmic and pulsating sounds in the movie "*The Last Temptation of Christ.*" I enter a tunnel with a bright light in the distance. I see a round wooden picture frame suspended by steel wires. In the middle of the frame is an almost featureless face. Who is it? As I fly closer, I think at first it is Hippocrates, then Galen. No, it isn't either. It must be someone with a vitally important message. Aristotle? Plato? Locke? Hume? Kant? Einstein? Jesus? I fly right by, and I can't be sure who it is until I look back, desperate to know. Suddenly I know. I don't know how; I just know. When I realize who I've just seen I start sobbing with joy.

'Slow down your breathing,' says Benjie.

The images have disappeared. I once again feel my arms, hands, fingers, legs, feet, and toes. Back on the green carpet in Maslow, I wipe the tears from my cheeks.

Gathering pillows from the side of the room, we sit in a circle, and Benjie invites us to share our experience. I jump in, eager to reveal my renewed encounter with God. Now I know he is within me.

In early childhood, it was easy to believe in biblical stories and to follow the traditional Orthodox religious and spiritual beliefs of my parents and teachers. My conflicts started when I tried to connect the complex mathematical and scientific realities of an evolving, ever-questioning, teenage brain with the three thousand-year-old set of stories and laws in the Five Books of Moses. This led to an explosive teenage rebellion against biblical truths when my beloved rabbi dismissed my questioning and told me I 'couldn't ask such questions until I was 40 years old.' Much to my father's dismay, I stopped attending synagogue services and developed a blind faith in science.

I cannot believe that in a matter of thirty minutes of "Holotropic Breathwork," which included guided imagery and evocative music, I have suddenly overturned years of doubt and I *know* the important truths. Like Saul on the road to Damascus, blinded by his discovery of Jesus and becoming Paul, I fell off my horse of scientific certainty. I get it. I am ready to begin my adventures into spiritual awareness.

Still with the mind of a scientist, I feel my first task is to find out what caused my awakening. I find a book on Holotropic Breathing at the Esalen bookstore. This is the beginning of a joyful and life-long exploration of "non-ordinary states of consciousness," a term coined by Stanislav Grof, a Czech-trained psychiatrist and psychoanalyst, and a pioneer in transpersonal psychology.

Grof had published papers on the serotonin-like effects of LSD on the human brain while at the Psychiatric Research Institute in his native Prague, and he continued his psychedelic research program at the Maryland Psychiatric Research Center and Johns Hopkins Medical School in the 1960's. By the late-sixties, especially after drug incidents in the psychology department at Harvard University, LSD research was no longer fundable, and he sought other methods that might mimic the hallucinogenic effects of mind-altering drugs. Some of his studies were done at Esalen when he was Scholar-in-Residence from 1973 to 1987.

He searched diverse ancient cultural and mystical practices known to induce states of spiritual ecstasy. These techniques included breathing, praying, hypnosis, sleep deprivation, fasting, music, and isolation tanks. Common to most spiritual practices were monotonous, repetitive musical chants with melodic, mathematically structured rhythms, known to enhance the human longing for truth, reality, immortality, peace, love, knowledge, and action.

Physiological, psychological, or pharmacological maneuvers or agents can give rise to altered states of consciousness, defined as any mental state which deviates from the normal waking state of consciousness that can affect physical and mental well-being.

Holotropic Breathwork was derived from various spiritual and pre-scientific traditions from around the world including Shamanism, Zen Yoga, T'ai Chi, Qigong, and Integrative Breathwork. It is a method of breath control that alters physiology through a combination of rapid breathing, evocative music, and guided imagery to putatively allow access to non-ordinary states of consciousness and into the therapeutic realm of self-awareness and spiritual healing.

During voluntary or involuntary rapid breathing, the amount of carbon dioxide removed from the lungs exceeds the body's production of the gas. This causes the concentration of carbon dioxide in the blood to fall. The body normally attempts to compensate for this hypocapnea by normal metabolic and biochemical mechanisms. If these normalizing efforts fail, a state of respiratory alkalosis, where the blood alkalinity increases, ensues, potentially resulting in the physical and behavioral effects that I had experienced.

Astounding associations occurred when research subjects were asked to draw mantras of their Holotropic state, and then to talk about them after emerging from the mystical breathing ritual. Many had detailed memories of intra-uterine life. Others reported experiencing a traumatic birth including frightening feelings of choking, difficulty breathing during birth, and passing through the dark tunnel of the birth canal. Many of the drawings highlighted suffering, death and dying, and revelations about a Higher Being – like my own Esalen experience. I had entered a lighted tunnel during my levitation journey, a common symbol of dying and passing into a heaven-like state.

I discovered several of Grof's writings that explained much of what I experienced. For example, he revealed that 'spiritual intelligence is the capacity to conduct our life in such a way that it reflects deep philosophical and metaphysical understanding of reality and of ourselves discovered through personal experiences during systematic spiritual pursuit.' Buddhist scriptures refer to this kind of spiritual wisdom as *prajna paramita* (transcendental wisdom). Unlike the dogmas of an organized church, spiritual intelligence acquired in the process of experiential self-exploration has the power to override the purely scientific worldview of material existence. At the same time, it is equally effective as a remedy against the fundamentalist misunderstanding and distortion of the spiritual message (Grof 2006).

Thomas Merton's observation addressed self-awareness when he said: 'What can we gain by sailing to the moon if we are not able to cross the abyss that separates us from ourselves.' He thought the attainment of self-awareness was the most important of all voyages of discovery.

I feel like I have discovered a pathway to my own enlightenment. I have been through a deep experiential journey which opened a pathway to what I believe will be extraordinary knowledge about myself, other people, various animals, nature and the universe. My journey during Holotropic Breathing has exposed me to the unconscious dynamics of my psyche. I have found that my perception of myself and of the world is influenced by forgotten or repressed memories from childhood, infancy, and long forgotten stories. I believe that I'm in the presence of a rich source of unique insights about the world I live in.

The first person with whom I share my Esalen workshop experience is Marianne. I telephone as soon as I can.

'I'm so grateful to you for sharing your love of Esalen with me. I think I understand why you're so wowed by this place.'

Now that I had journeyed into a vastly different territory and experienced a state of unaccountable energy and imagination, I am anxious to learn more and to share every experience with her. I describe everything that I had discovered and reminisce on my academic need to prove everything by pure scientific evidence. While I'm aware of keeping boundaries between former patients and doctors, I see no harm in sharing my experiences at Esalen.

'Maybe you will understand that there are other ways for people to heal,'

She thinks that it might be helpful to begin to use more intuition in everything that I do, including taking care of patients like her. She knows from her experience how important our team was in her treatment. But there was a big void afterwards that was filled by spiritual and mystical healing, things that she learned from Esalen. Only now, after my experience, am I able to understand what she meant.

I return to my surgical practice in Michigan unsure of how I will function as a clinical scientist.

CHAPTER EIGHT:

၏လ

MOVING TOWARDS MY AUTHENTIC SELF

As the plane takes off from Monterey airport I start to cry again as I look south toward Esalen, feeling like I have left my soul there, a place of miracle healing. I board the connecting flight from San Francisco to Detroit with mixed feelings, looking forward to seeing my family, but sad to leave Esalen. During the flight, I continue reading Grof's book, "The adventure of self-discovery," searching specifically for sections on holotropic therapy, finding that thousands of people had reported stories like mine. Similar experiences have been reported by research subjects under the influence of the drug LSD, including vivid new feelings and awareness of smells, sounds, colors, feelings and emotions.

I feel a strange new slowness mixed with uncertainty, an ethereal rawness, as if the monomaniacal world of surgery and science has suddenly been eroded by an extra-ordinary tranquility, somewhat like a Le Mans racing driver might feel after driving at two hundred miles per hour and suddenly stopping, mounting a camel, and walking slowly around the race track. Yet there is a part of me that is still travelling around in my head at enormous speed. That speed of my prior life is now in conflict with my new need to stop and appreciate the beauty of nature and to watch my breathing. As we fly over the Sierra Nevada Mountains to the right of the plane, I see a breathtaking sight of snow-covered peaks covered in dazzling sunlight. I'm overcome with the beauty and, once again, the floodgates open and tears pour down my cheeks.

Abby, aged eight, and Ali, six, come running to the back door of my house as soon as they hear my key in the lock. They are right there and, as soon as they see me, they grab me and hug me and won't let go. I kiss them and immediately start sobbing. Bewildered, they hug my thighs, interspersing themselves between me and my wife, usually bubbly and talkative, but now also puzzled, wondering what has happened to the man who hardly ever shows his emotions. I catch my breath, compose myself as much as I can, sit on the living room sofa with one kid on either side of me, listen to them as they excitedly cram many experiences that I have missed during my absence into a cascade of chatter, a torrent of words, demonstrations of new school projects and stories, and a dress for a play that Abby is doing on Sunday.

I want so much to tell them about my experience but I'm uncertain, still trying to process my thoughts and ideas. I tell them a little about the vegetable and flower gardens, the views of the Pacific Ocean below the cliff, the unique hot springs and baths, the dining room, the whales swimming nearby, and about my fellow workshop attendees, while leaving out the strange details of my holotropic journey. After an hour of sharing and talking they leave and go to bed.

Now it is just me and Jerrilyn and I try to talk about what happened to me over the past week. It is just a mere fifty-six hours since my Esalen explosion and I need to talk about the change that it has brought to me, a change that feels overwhelming because it has taken away the certainty of my life, leaving in its place an uneasy void of the unknown, a place where I had not allowed myself to go in my clinical or personal life, where I had to be decisive and certain. My internal journey needs time to evolve, and I need to examine my feelings and emotions as I work out where to go next.

I sit down at my new Apple computer, just barely three weeks out of the box, the workings of which I'm only now beginning to understand a little, playing with the software that will enable me to write down my experiences, searching the words and sentences for the meaning that I'm now so curious to unravel, writing everything about what has just happened at Esalen, knowing that I'm in an almost delirious state of mind, something akin to a spiritual emergency, alert to everything around me, the colors outside the house in

Franklin, Michigan, of the late winter, dreary and grey compared to the greenery and flowers of Esalen. I write for hours, through the night into the next morning, almost without a break, using a stream of consciousness where I write everything that comes to mind, typing with my untrained 'hunt and peck' style on the keyboard, page upon page streaming from my brain onto the computer screen, miraculously preserved *in silico* by the touch of a finger hitting 'save.'

I still feel alert at 6.42 am as the sun rises, awake and still writing endless words, sentences, paragraphs and pages, reluctant to stop and unwilling to sleep. I haven't eaten or drunk anything for at least nine hours, and I don't feel hungry or thirsty. I try a little breakfast cereal and a glass of orange juice, but I feel nauseated, unable to finish even half of a bowl. I walk around the house, looking out the windows of the living room, yearning for green leaves, flowers, a blue sky, the Pacific Ocean, and, seeing none, I head back to my computer in my home office. The early morning seems to rush by as I hear the rest of the inhabitants of the household stirring and giggling and beginning their day.

Sunday morning, a time for me take the family to brunch at a nearby restaurant, and we bundle up and get into my car. The snow on the ground, white and clean in our suburban neighborhood, seems too bright, an overpowering intrusion into my sunglasses-covered eyes. The subdivision is quiet enough but, soon, I ease south onto a car-filled Telegraph Avenue, traffic noises permeating through my senses, and I feel overwhelmed by the sights and the sounds, contrasting abrasively with the tranquil quiet of the Maslow room at Esalen. I park the car and the kids are expectant, looking forward to a lovely brunch at the deli, hidden at the back of a large parking lot in a three-story building south of Thirteen Mile road. I want to be in the communal dining room at Esalen with no parking lots or cars, and without the traffic noises, rambunctious deli patrons, occasional raucous laughter, screaming children, nauseating smells of scrambled eggs and bacon, and bottomless cups of coffee. The food is served, and my nausea grows, and I cannot eat the processed food, a great contrast to the fresh fruit, vegetables, salads, home-baked multigrain bread, grapes off the vine, and farm-fresh eggs at Esalen.

I manage to get through the restaurant experience, and we head home to prepare for Abby's afternoon play. Looking through my copious mail while the family gets ready for the afternoon adventure, I find a Fedex package from work, delivered in my absence, containing a thick wad of papers for the

Research Committee meeting tomorrow at the Dearborn Inn. I look through the agenda and notice a proposal that I must read and critique as a primary reviewer. Normally I relish the challenge and I love to pick at defects in the hypotheses, specific aims, background studies, introduction, and proposed statistical analyses. I regard my presence on the committee of twenty senior scientists and clinicians at Henry Ford Health System as a recognition of my scientific skills and integrity. But today, knowing that I will need to embed myself in the project later this afternoon, and print a review that will be distributed to other members tomorrow, I feel a refreshed bout of nausea and panic. I don't want this. I want to be outside in the Big Sur mountains, forests, and beaches, listening to the sounds of nature, seeing the beauty and the colors, smelling the uniqueness of fresh cut grass, and the atmosphere permeated by the gently rolling waves of the Pacific Ocean.

Doing the review and writing the critique is quite difficult but I dig deep into my tenacious spirit and I manage to do the reading and writing on time. If I think this is difficult it is nothing compared to my day with the committee in a spacious dining room at the Dearborn Inn on Monday.

I've had many meetings over the past two years with the accomplished group of men and women, leaders in the institution, who I respect. We love talking to each other when we meet. Today I see things about my colleagues that shock and surprise me. I see hard-working, striving professionals, with bulging egos. I had known about those egos before and I had thought them to be good and necessary.

None of us get to serve on this kind of committee without an ego. But my experience last week at Esalen has exposed me to my own ego and I want to get rid of it altogether. I can't do that today and I feel flushed, flummoxed and insecure when my time comes to present my review. My hesitancy seems to expose my uncertainty and I'm a little embarrassed.

Reticence is not an attribute that is welcome in this environment and I must push through it, gaining strength as I read the paperwork I prepared yesterday. My newly identified ability to see myself and my ego fights with my old me that didn't see that the ego, interferes with my tranquility and happiness. I seem to be confronting my demons.

Fred Hetzel, a research collaborator with a PhD in Physics, a friend and sometime confidant, smart and remarkably sure that the world is all pragmatic and understandable in scientific terms, is well versed in scientific observation and analysis and yet he doesn't have a clue that I'm in a kind of emotional crisis. I've been on a baffling journey and I cannot talk to him about it. I cannot tell anyone about it. I must process my feelings and work out myself what happened to me.

The day with the Research Committee passes and I don't believe anyone in the room could really tell that every moment in the day is a near crisis for me. I have not eaten all day, drinking only water, and conversations are troubling. I can't concentrate as well as I usually do, my mind pulling me back to the tranquility of Esalen and my new friends from last week.

It is Tuesday morning and I've been back at work for one day, an unusual day because I don't spend a lot of time in committees. I spend my time in my laboratory, or in the clinic or in the operating room. Today I have a case to do in the OR and I'm terrified. I'm newly familiar with the ego and I believe that a surgeon cannot function in the OR without an abundance of ego.

How can I do any surgical procedure without a strong ego? Surely, I need that ego to allow me to bark orders at scrub technicians, talk sharply to the surgical resident working with me, teach the medical student the anatomy that I unravel under the bright OR lights, and do an elegant procedure?

I take in a deep breath and practice watching my breathing like I had learned last week during the holotropic breathing experience before I greet the patient in the pre-operative area.

The OR lights look too bright. The usual noises of the OR seem too loud. People are moving too quickly. I see the unhappy ones with sullen faces as they push wheeled gurneys and patients wearing OR gowns, IV bags hanging on poles, oxygen tanks tucked safely away in case they are urgently needed, down corridors crowded with equipment, supplies and trolleys, the OR numbers hanging from the ceiling and I find my way to my room. I'm so used to this experience but today is different because I'm acutely aware of the unhappy ones, people who I might previously not have noticed, or at least not noticed that they were unhappy.

I'm unsure of my ability to do the case but somehow, despite my altered mental state, the rhythm of the OR kicks in and I do the technical side of the procedure perfectly well.

I'm acutely aware that I feel differently about the resident helping me, the medical student on my side of the table, the patient we are about to operate on, the anesthesiologist giving drugs at the head of the table, and all the other people in the room. I don't feel the same sense of domination and superiority that I felt previously.

My surgical culture, which promotes a strong, individually oriented ethos, continues to unconsciously emphasize the illusion of an authority that demands domination. But now I see the idea of power in the OR as quite unsound. I have come to realize, because of my experience last week at Esalen, that I had previously been sucked into a power dynamic which persuaded me into believing that, because I am an authority, that I am better than everyone else. I now realize that the attitude of power that I previously demonstrated might well have made my patients and my team feel less, or weaker, than me.

Like Scrooge, he after a night of dreams and flying around London, me after a holotropically-inspired flying journey, I seem to have awakened to everyone else's needs, and I feel a new sense of awe, an agape love of everyone in the room. I have come to believe that everyone has the divine within them.

The operation is done in the same technical way that I had managed in my prior days in the OR but with me talking gently and kindly to everyone. I address everyone by their first name, requesting instruments and saying 'please.' I'm not sure if they notice the difference but I feel good. During slow periods in the four-hour operation I concentrate as much on what I'm doing but I tell stories about myself and my family, intended to lighten the atmosphere.

Why didn't I think about this before? I'm letting everyone know that I'm human and that I acknowledge them as human. I invite them to talk about their families because I want to know, and they will hopefully feel at ease with me.

I must see a patient in the hospital that I had operated upon before going to Esalen. She has not been able to eat and is receiving intra-venous nutrition and has been in the hospital for over two weeks. My partners had done everything possible to find out why her bowel wasn't functioning properly, including many x-rays and blood tests, and there continues to be no good reason for this ongoing complication. She seems otherwise quite well, awake, aware, breathing normally, but with a nasogastric tube still aspirating large amounts of greenish fluid every day. Her intestine has seemingly adopted a lazy stance and is just not moving. This is not a mechanical obstruction which I could fix by an operation.

Cathie, my nurse, is exasperated because this delayed recovery doesn't follow the text-book post-operative pattern. We all want to move on, take out the nasogastric tube, feed the patient normally and have her go home.

'I'm going to try something different with you. A technique that I believe will work. But it requires intense concentration and a belief that not everything we do in Western medicine is the only way to heal patients. Are you willing to work with me?'

The patient is confused, and Cathie looks quizzically at me. I'm not sure where to go with this but I want to try something I learned last week, a form of guided imagery, a way to influence the mind.

'Ok. If it doesn't hurt and you think it is safe. What do I need to do?'

'Close your eyes. Relax and breathe.

Ok, good.

In and out.

Now a little faster.

Great.

Keep going. Keep your eyes closed.

I want you to watch your breath going into your lungs.

Feel the oxygen going in and out.

Breath deeper still. Breath faster.

Watch the oxygen travel from your lungs,

in the blood vessels,

into your heart,

out into the blood vessels traveling to your gut.

Good.

Keep going.

Now, in your mind, look at your stomach,

and your duodenum

and your small intestine.

Breath faster.

Imagine that you're caressing your gut, urging and coaxing it to start moving again.

Great.

Now start to slowly breath normally.

Ok open your eyes.'

She looks fine and relaxed and I tell her that we'll watch over the next day, that I hope this will help her gut get over its reticence to move.

On Wednesday, she has a bowel movement, I hear evidence with my stethoscope that her small bowel is moving, and the nasogastric suction is markedly diminished. On Thursday, we remove the NG tube and start feeding her a fluid diet. On Friday, she is ready to go home.

I tell Cathie to tell no one about the details of this experiment. It may just be coincidence that her full recovery was related in time to my Guided Imagery.

I remember a story my mother told me as a young child about an unconventional healing. My mother loved to tell stories about illnesses in our relatives, her friends and herself. I loved to listen. She told us about her mother's bout with typhoid in 1907, which she survived at a time when there were no antibiotics. She talked extensively about her father's diabetes and showed me grandpa's urine sugar testing kit in the bathroom at his cottage in Brakpan. She told us how her older brother, Abe, died from peritonitis at age nineteen. Every time I got a tummy ache I was terrified that I too might get peritonitis and die. But her favorite story was about her own recovery from peritonitis in 1936.

She was a high-school senior, living in a dormitory at a Catholic girl's school seventy miles from home, and extremely ill. The nuns contacted my grandfather, Chaim, who went to pick her up and brought her to the Far East Rand Hospital in Springs, a few miles from Brakpan where he had a flourishing hardware store adjacent to the booming gold mining properties, and where he and grandma Taube and their children lived. Mom was critically ill, and the local doctor told my grandparents that she would likely die. My grandfather, who had already lost one child to peritonitis, and several children to miscarriages, contacted my grandmother's cousin, Percy Peltz, a specialist gynecologist trained in Edinburgh, Scotland, and with a growing practice in Johannesburg. Percy examined my mother and told my grandfather that there wasn't much hope of recovery.

'You operate now!' he had demanded in his thick Lithuanian accent.

Years later when I was doing a medical student rotation with him, I asked Percy about this episode. He told me that my grandfather wouldn't accept 'no' as the answer. He operated on her and found that she had generalized peritonitis, a condition with a very high mortality rate at that time. He had placed rubber drains in her abdomen to drain the infection and went out to explain to my grandfather that there wasn't much hope of survival. He also told him my mother would never have children if she survived.

'My grandmother saved me,' my mother said.

At four feet eleven inches, my mother's Bobba (grandmother), a lively woman full of grit and determination, and always dressed in dark clothes, thick stockings and with a black head scarf, ruled the kitchen. My mother, lying in bed and delirious with fever and sepsis, was barely conscious when Bobba barged into her room and covered her completely with a heavy fur coat and chanted prayers in Yiddish. The next day mom was better, and she continued to improve and eventually went home.

Many believed that it was the fur coat that did it and the story continued for decades that tiny 'Bobba' had saved my mother's life using a remedy from the 'old country.'

Now, following my levitation experience, and for the first time in my life, I thought maybe there was something more to the 'granny story.'

CHAPTER NINE:

❧

PATIENTS AS FRIENDS

U nlike most scientists with PhDs running labs, I run my lab like a surgeon, doing 'rounds' every day, studying every fine detail of the data accumulated since yesterday, criticizing everything that doesn't seem to fit my hypotheses, planning the experiments for the next day.

Lisa, a bright, motivated, Japanese-American lab assistant, and Patty, a quiet, careful, thoughtful, Mexican-American woman, who I hired after she spent the summer with me between her Junior and Senior years at the University of Detroit, Mercy, are happy to meet every day and discuss their experiments. They are meticulous, and I am never completely happy with their results because that's the way it goes with lab experiments, only 5 to 10 percent of them working perfectly. But now I'm different and I learn from my experience at Esalen and my transformation to believing that each of the people I work with has the divine within them. I must continue what I learned; to love what is mortal, to hold it carefully and, when the time comes, to let it go completely. I must consciously cultivate the awakening I've experienced and share it with those that I work with.

It makes life very different when I walk around and greet everyone warmly. Everyone. Every day. As expected, some people are suspicious of this new behavior, but many welcome my new warmth and friendliness. I'm also able to see every new patient as another human needing my help. It is magical to see the divine within everyone and to feel whole heartedly loving, no matter how I am treated. I feel good when I accomplish big surgeries without yelling at a junior resident for not moving quickly enough or failing to complete notes in a timely fashion. I patiently tolerate mistakes and gently describe ways to improve.

Howard Terebelo, an oncologist friend, calls me late one afternoon while I'm on call for emergency general surgery cases. His father-in-law is downstairs in the Emergency Department. Saul has severe pain in his right upper abdomen, and he is slightly yellow. We do the appropriate tests and he has a large gall stone in the gallbladder. His liver enzymes show that he has a little bit of liver damage. I recommend that we operate on him to remove his gallbladder.

In addition to the inflamed gallbladder with stones, he has an early form of cirrhosis which we discover is caused by taking massive doses of the vitamin, niacin. On patient rounds in the hospital with the resident I teach in the so-called Socratic way, by asking questions and, when getting an answer, asking other questions. I do this around the Saul's bed, and he appears to be unconscious, on a respirator and drugged, not responding to questions or to light physical stimuli. It takes two days for him to wake up enough to breathe on his own after the surgery. On the third day, he smiles at me, beaming from ear to ear, and shakes my hand, thanking me for doing such a great job, helping him get over the pain of cholecystitis. On the fourth post-operative day, he gives me a gift, a tiny copy of Shakespeare's play 'Henry V.' Inscribed in the front are a few words that show that he is so thankful and that he recognizes in me a person of quality who will appreciate this masterpiece. I'm very touched by this demonstration of kindness and love.

Two weeks later, discharged and recovering at home, he sees me in the outpatient clinic. He is doing well, his wound healed, and he's eating normally. We discuss his niacin intake, and negotiate his cutting down of the vitamin, with the hope that his early cirrhosis, caused by this habit, will disappear and heal. He is discharged from the clinic; there's no need for him to see me again.

But he wants to linger for a while, asking questions about me and my training and then about my family, talking about the political figures from Southern Africa he had met as a newspaper editor, probing my ideas about the Apartheid Government. I keep looking at my watch but that doesn't stop him. I firmly but politely tell him I have other patients waiting for me and he leaves.

Two weeks later he's back. I'm a little worried that something bad has happened but he seems fine. Not that I hadn't enjoyed our conversation but there's really no time for these conversations in the clinic. So, my initial reaction is one of dismay. I walk into the examining room and he greets me with a warm smile.

'What's happening?' I ask. He has some vague complaints and I stop him.

All he wants to do is talk to me, to find out about my family, my origins and my political views. He wants to know about my time in South Africa. He seems lonely.

'I tell you what,' I say. 'How about we meet for coffee at the end of my clinic day? That way we can talk and not worry that we're holding up other patients in the clinic.'

'I have a better idea. Why don't I treat you to lunch?'

I'm a little hesitant to do this. My teachers in medical school, residency and fellowship training had warned about maintaining barriers between patients and doctors. They believed that one had to maintain an emotional distance. In my former mode, as a person of authority with important work to do, I was rigidly protective of my privacy and would not have befriended a patient. I have changed because of Marianne, although meeting her for a meal seemed alright because she was no longer my patient. I think about how that lunch with her led me to Esalen and a transformative experience. Perhaps meeting Saul for lunch will be good for both of us. He's interested in my South African origins because he's a historian and philosopher, and he briefly edited a local liberal newspaper and is interested in African-American causes. I reason he is no longer my patient. The only day I can count on a 45-minute window of time for lunch is Tuesday. He jumps at the opportunity.

So, before Mitch Albom's famous book and movie, 'Tuesdays with Morrie,' I have my 'Tuesdays with Saul.' We meet every Tuesday for years. I learn a great deal from Saul and his wife, Ruth. They are a highly educated couple and my family enjoys meeting them. They impart some of the wisdom about American life that I, a foreign-born surgeon, need.

An unusual event early in our friendship, seals our relationship for life.

After operating all day, I go to my locker to change out of my OR greens. The locker has been forcibly opened and my clothes stolen, including my wallet. It is bad enough that my license and credit cards are gone. They can be replaced. But my 1887 Victorian half-crown is also gone. I am devastated. My father had given it to me when I left South Africa in 1975. His father had given it to him in 1933, just before he died.

He brought it on his journey to South Africa, from Lithuania, through England, in 1902. He kept it as a symbol of good luck. When he gave it to my father, he told him that it should pass on to the oldest boy in the family.

I tell Saul the terrible news about the silver coin and he understands my grief. We talk about my grandfather and his family.

Three months later when we meet for lunch Saul beams from ear to ear as he places a small gift-wrapped box on the table in front of me.

'What's this?' I ask.

'Open it,' he says triumphantly.

Inside is an 1887 silver Victorian half-crown that he found through a numismatist in Ontario, an exact replica of my grandfather's coin.

This act of friendship further melts my surgical façade and I realize again how precious it is to interact on a human level with a patient. I tell my residents about this act of kindness. I encourage them to establish friendships with select patients.

Tom, a strapping thirty-seven-year old engineer at the Ford Motor Company, had a melanoma of his flank excised by me, as well as lymph nodes in his groin that showed the tumor had spread there. Following surgery, nine months of interferon immuno-therapy for metastatic melanoma, enough to disable a horse, had turned his hair grey, and caused him to develop splotchy skin depigmentation, vitiligo, probably a sign that he had developed antibodies to melanin, a pigment found in melanoma cells, and reduced his familiar exuberance. The following year we discovered the melanoma had spread to his lungs. Two months of interleukin 2, given to him at the Karmanos Cancer Center, part of Wayne State University Medical Center, failed to affect the tumors.

His parents had driven from North Dakota to be with their son.

'Doc, can you help us? The doctors at the Cancer Center told us the treatment isn't working and there is no other treatment and that he has no more than a few months to live.'

A desperate situation and one that no physician wants to own. I talk apologetically about the poor results of standard therapy, but his father cuts me short.

'Do you have children, doctor?'

'Yes.'

'We're just simple folk. We don't know what to do. What would you do if this was your son?'

'I guess I'd find the most promising research program and go for it.'

'Where is that?'

I tell them about Dr Rosenberg at the Surgery Branch of the National Cancer Institute. He has several Phase 1 studies for melanoma and one of them seems quite promising.

'How do we get into his program?' asks Tom.

I see the divine in him and his parents. I put myself into their shoes. This is my time to do something that might help, although the chances are small of that happening. If I do nothing he will certainly die within a few months. His medical oncologist, the one that I referred him to, is renowned for his management of stage IV melanoma. He has told Tom that there is no other treatment available. I strongly believe in the possibility that influencing the immune system may be of help for Tom.

'Give me a few minutes and I'll call them.'

Fortunately, Tom fits the criteria for the study, and he goes to Bethesda. The NCI team take a sample of his tumor and his peripheral blood mononuclear cells and culture them for a month in interleukin 2. They gave him his proliferating autologous immune cells back by one intravenous injection and add interleukin infusions. He has very mild side effects.

Two months later the follow-up CT scan shows no evidence of tumor in his lungs.

Tom visits me every six months and I receive notes from Dr Rosenberg's team at regular intervals. There is no evidence of recurrence.

Twelve years have passed after his treatment. He doesn't need to see me, but he wants to come back. I think part of this is because he feels so lucky and grateful for my suggestion to see Dr Rosenberg. I saw the divine in him, and I still do. He is a fabulous young man, vigorous, caring thoughtful and strong, and he managed to get through all the treatments and follow up he needed. He loves to tell me how grateful he is for his life. He pulls out his cell-phone and proudly shows me a picture of his new bride. He met a wonderful young woman, shared his story and found an empathetic soul to share his life. Here is evidence of a divine miracle, a man who has survived an awful disease and I feel somehow part of this lovely story.

A year later he shows me a picture of his new son, a beautiful child, perfect in every way.

Sometimes we can save people from the jaws of death and the result can be miraculous new life.

Living with an incurable malignancy obviously takes a toll and even strong personalities eventually break down. Like the Sword of Damocles, the inevitable hangs over ones' head day and night. In his professional life, Joe, a tough, retired Canton policeman, faced possible death every day in his job. Handgun drawn, walking slowly and deliberately into a dangerous situation with an armed and dangerous felon, he would have been in an acute state of 'flight or fight.' Sudden death could come in seconds or minutes. He would know how to act. He had trained to do that. It was his job. He had been there before – even been shot at once or twice, bullets whizzing past his head. The 'event' passed, and the guy was in his patrol car, handcuffed and heading to the police station. Another successful night in the never-ending fight against evil.

But melanoma lurking in the cop's body? It didn't care whether he was a hero or not. Or whether he was a great guy. It could strike any time. He can't look for the tumor behind a door or in a closet. He can read a medical textbook and that might tell him where those loitering malignant cells might be lying dormant, but they are too small to feel or see. They are microscopic. They might be anywhere. Then–boom! They grow, almost overnight, and he might feel the tumor. Or the scan would find them when he can't feel them. He can't arrest the tumor and put it in handcuffs. He can't hall it off to jail.

He can't draw his gun when the tumors come. He can't strike them with his fist.

His parents taught him to rely on himself. He feels helpless and he hates relying on me. We do surgery, or gave him a promising new drug, and the tumor disappears. Yet again. But it will come back. He knows that. We just can't tell when that will be, and he knows I can't tell him either.

And he is the strong one, in charge when his children need him. Or his elderly mother. Or his wife. Or his friends at the church he attends. He has come through for them, and for the neighbors when they have a problem. Everyone knows they can rely on Joe. But he is unable to avoid the recurrent tumors.

Twenty years after I performed an inguino-femoral lymphadenectomy for melanoma of his right leg, and about forty subsequent operations for in-transit metastases of cutaneous and subcutaneous leg and thigh lesions, and radiation therapy for one of the deep lesions close to the bone, and hyperthermic perfusion with chemotherapy, the tumor has finally metastasized to his right external iliac nodes. It had passed that barrier that we had talked about – the inguinal ligament. While confined to his lower extremity we had controlled it with local therapies. For fifteen years, while we fought this disease together, while sharing stories about our lives, and playing golf, doctor and patient on the golf course together, while seeing him at least every four months for his disease, we both knew that there was always a strong likelihood that the tumor would metastasize to the inside of his body. We both knew that there were no good melanoma treatments in the 1990s other than surgery.

We treat this new tumor with a new targeted therapy drug, one that is directed at a gene mutation which his tumor expresses.

Joe is visibly moved as I show him his latest PET-CT scan and he hugs me and my nurse, Susie. The targeted therapy has worked and the lesion in his pelvis is controlled. The relief is palpable and joyful, and he wipes the tears from his cheeks, composes himself, looks me in the eyes, shakes my hand, and walks out to the parking lot, a dignified man, a jewel of a person. We have been there before, and he will be back.

'Do you play golf, Doctor,' Don asked during one of his many visits to my clinic.

And I mean 'many.' By that time, I had operated on him at least ten times in fifteen years for recurrent low grade liposarcoma of the spermatic cord. He loves golf and tennis and he is back on the golf course within a day or two of excisional surgery in the perineum. I cannot hold him back while I imagine the worst possible complications.

Most other patients with similar operations in that 'delicate' part of the anatomy would not venture very far and try not to walk much until the pain is gone. Not Don. An exuberant, jovial man with an Irish pedigree, he cannot be held back by any discomfort. He golfs the day after surgery! He loves people. Indeed, he loves most things with an unmatched passion. He must keep his dates with his buddies on the golf course, no matter what.

'I haven't played in years,' I reply.

'There are so many great South African golfers. I bet you play well.'

I explain that I had started playing at age 5. My uncle had a golf course and I was quite good by the time I was a teenager. But medical school and surgical residency had not allowed me the consistent time I needed to continue playing well and I'd elected to give up the game. I hadn't played in twelve years.

'I want you to be my guest at Oakland Hills. Can you make it next Saturday?'

How can I refuse such an offer to play on one of the country's top golf courses? So, I accept the offer.

He wants to play for money! 'OK. Five bucks.'

The first hole is a disaster. The only thing I don't do is hit the ball out of bounds.

The second hole isn't much better.

But the third hole makes Don look at me curiously. I chip the ball from the bunker directly into the hole for a par. I keep improving and we are neck and neck when I hit a beautiful drive 250 yards straight down the 18th fairway. My second shot lands just short of the green. I sink the ball with my third shot. An eagle!

Don looks at me and smiles. 'Doctor, I want you to promise me you won't tell anyone in the clubhouse how you beat me.'

'Sure. No problem.'

We meet a few of Don's friends in the immaculate clubhouse change room. He introduces me as 'his doctor.'

'He's the greatest doc ever. But he told me he hadn't played golf for years. Yeah, sure! You should have seen him on the eighteenth hole. Can you believe he shot an eagle? What do you think I should do with his medical advice? Should I believe a guy who leads me astray on the golf course and takes my money?'

Lots of guffaws and backslapping follow as we head for the bar.

Befriending patients turns into a caring event from both sides. The patient cares about me and I care about the him.

Don continues to develop recurrences in the perineum and, as sometimes happens with this type of liposarcoma, the latest one, a rapidly growing recurrence in the perineum, has finally grown back to the point that I can no longer operate on him. Chemotherapy doesn't work. Radiation gains us a few months before it grows beyond the treatment of anything we have.

Something happens at this point between Don and me. I have been his savior and his friend. He had confidence that we would beat this horrible disease and, for twenty years, we had managed to keep him going. He had 'shown me off' to his family and friends, inviting me to his house on the lake, where I met his friends and family, had fun swimming and barbecuing, and Don had continually told everyone what a great doctor I am. There was never a thought by him that the tumor would grow beyond my control.

I'm always cautious about sounding too optimistic when dealing with a potentially lethal malignant tumor. But the gregarious Don, who has a large appetite for the good things in life, a man well known in the Detroit area, perhaps the most optimistic person ever, a man who quickly bounced back to life even after his beloved wife died unexpectedly in her mid-seventies, was not the kind of man I could talk to seriously about death from this tumor. Provided the tumor recurred locally, in the area where it started, and did not spread to any important internal organs, where it could threaten his life, I could not realistically talk negatively to him. But now the inevitable has happened. It has recurred in a way where I must address a pessimistic option to an optimist.

Since he isn't about to give up, he suddenly turns cold on me. Just like in any loving and caring relationship, such as when siblings turn on each other in adulthood and never talk to each other again, or when a marriage turns sour, or when business partners vehemently and assertively disagree with each other, all resulting from polarized misunderstandings, so Don no longer trusts my medical opinion. He seeks opinions at the University of Michigan, forty-five miles to our west, and the experts in soft tissue tumors there are unable to offer him an alternative treatment.

Even wonderful optimists like Don must sometimes come to the realization that death is approaching. Palliative management of the inoperable tumor is horrendous for him and for me as he returns, a changed man but needing my help for pain control and wound management. He refuses hospice care as he deteriorates. Watching him suffer is very difficult for me and for his family. Like a beached whale he struggles daily while his daughters watch and wait for the inevitable. The worst sight I have emblazoned on my brain is seeing him finally unable to walk, wheeled into my clinic by his daughter, Maureen. Take away a man's independence and his soul and face look downwards, the joviality gone, silence pervades, and one almost wishes that we could summon the angel of death. Eventually, thankfully, the time comes, and the misery is mostly gone, replaced by a sense of relief that the great man is finally done suffering. We can once more celebrate the life of a joyful person, remembering his stories and his wonderful smile.

Sometimes caring turns into something unexpected

Chapter Ten:

❧

Creativity and Curiosity

I am driven by a passion for novelty, the solving of the old challenges and the desire to create new ones, to look at the world around me, to see how it is, and to imagine other possibilities that are not immediately obvious. My experience at Esalen has enhanced my creativity enabling me to more astutely imagine possibilities in my mind and converting them into reality. I believe that creators manipulate and reconfigure existing ideas and forms. Creativity is often no more than rearranging ideas.

I dream about discovering why breast cancer cells spread and kill my patients. Within the 100 billion neurons and the 100 trillion neuronal connections in my brain there must be a creative idea that I can work with to find a way to prevent and treat breast cancer cells from metastasizing to the lymph nodes in the armpit. I've been doing lab research on this subject since the 1970's, presenting my findings at scientific meetings and publishing papers, each one adding a small amount of information but the total picture, the finite answers, always seem hidden. I have not yet been able to cobble together a clear picture of the processes involved. There are too many unknowns.

Creative people who succeed in initiating a new understanding of anything in the world, from great artistic achievements like the Sistine Chapel frescoes of Michelangelo, to the musical innovations of Beethoven, or Alexander Fleming's discovery of penicillin, or the literary masterpieces of Shakespeare, or the great leap forward produced by Watson and Crick establishing DNA structure-where did their creative genius originate and how can I create something entirely original? I cannot do it alone; I must know all there is to know of the existing information by studying prior innovators.

My Marianne-induced transformation has enabled me to think more clearly about my patients and, every time I operate on a breast cancer or melanoma patient, and I find the sentinel node by injection of a radio-tracer around the tumor in the skin or in the breast, I think about tumor cells entering a lymphatic trunk, a tube-shaped structure, that normally carries fluid from one part of the body to the neighboring lymph nodes. I imagine that I'm swimming alongside tiny molecules and cells as they try to find a way to leave the cancer site to travel far away to another part of the body. Why do they want to leave a place that provides them all the nutrition and oxygen they need, provided free of charge by the patient's blood vessels, to seek other places to live, places in the body that might not be as hospitable to their survival?

In a sense, I had metastasized from South Africa to the USA and I left a place of comfort, my home, which provided me a livelihood, good nutrition, water, oxygen, family, friends and a comfortable future. I, too, found a way to travel to a potentially inhospitable place, where I established a foothold. I traveled by planes, trains, automobiles and boats; tumor cells travel through tubes filled with fluid. My travel required me to acquire a Green Card, a visa, and buying a plane ticket. I arrived at JFK airport after a trans-Atlantic flight. I passed through customs agents in New York, who endorsed my entry into the country because I had been approved by Immigration Authorities. From there I could go anywhere in the country. I had permission.

Tumor cells travel to other organs in the body without approval of the patient. They simulate an invasive species, like uninvited Ukrainian mussels, hitching a ride on ships keels, turbines and propellers, finding a new home in Lake Michigan where they decimate the plankton so important for the health of the water and its natural species that had survived harsh winters and scorching summers, only to succumb to the foreign mollusks.

A perennial question about tumor cells and their patterns of metastasis, one that has plagued scientists for decades, is the potentially different anatomic pathways adopted by tumor cells seeking to travel to internal organs. There are different schools of thought: some believe the tumor cells enter the blood vessels in and around a primary tumor and travel to distant sites, entry points akin to the on-ramps of major freeways that would allow an automobile driver to travel anywhere, stopping along the way for gas and an occasional meal, until a more permanent place is reached to set up a home in which to live. But there is still a possibility that tumor cells can only enter the blood vessels after first traveling to the lymph nodes. Which of these is true? Here is my chance to be creative, to come up with original ideas that might change the way we understand a biological principle.

I need data from experiments to reorganize the ideas from prior observations by many clinical and lab scientists. The ideas that I work with originated in the nineteenth century based on studies in cancer patients by Virchow, a nineteenth century German physician, famous for his observations on the origins of cells and his finding that stomach cancer can spread to a lymph node in the left side of the neck. Surgical treatments for breast and other cancers were developed in the early twentieth century based upon Virchow's universally accepted ideas that tumors spread to internal organs only after first spreading to lymph nodes.

Bernard Fisher in Pittsburgh in the mid to late twentieth century rearranged Virchow's ideas based on his own experiments and those of others, the arguments so compelling that he changed the paradigm of thinking. He did not dispute the observed fact that breast cancers sometimes spread to lymph nodes in the armpit. He quoted the observations of pathologists who reported seeing tumor cells were directly inside small vessel capillaries in and around the primary breast cancer, and suggested they could directly invade those vessels right there; he and others had no doubt those capillaries were blood vessels, clinching the argument that they did not need to travel to the lymph nodes first to gain access to the blood circulation. But this argument was not convincing because later research showed those vessels containing tumor cells were lymphatics, not blood vessels, which enabled cells direct access to the lymph nodes in the armpit.

The more I thought about my observations versus those of Fisher, a surgeon like me but already revered by oncologists world-wide, the more I became convinced that my findings, in both mouse and human experiments, supported the findings of Virchow one hundred years before I was born.

This created a predicament for me because I was completely unknown and few people read my published papers from the work I did in my lab and in my clinic.

I'm able to think better since my Esalen experience and this will help me discover the mechanisms by which breast cancer cells travel to organs inside the body.

CHAPTER ELEVEN:

～～～

CARING

The belief that I should be a compassionate and caring person before I could claim to be an empathetic clinician started when I was a child.

'How do you feel?' my mother asked as she gently combed my hair with a brush and washed my face with a warm wash cloth. 'Does your back hurt? Let's close the window so you don't catch cold. How does your back feel?'

'It hurts a little, mom.'

Just two days after the pediatrician, Dr Stanley Javett, injected purified protein derivative into the skin of my upper back and covered the site with an Elastoplast bandage we were back in his office in Hillbrow. He pulled the dressing off, looked at the injected site, covered it with a fresh Band Aid and wrote a note in my chart.

'Mrs Nathanson the PPD test is positive. This means he has been exposed to tuberculosis. David's six weeks of coughing that brought you here in the first place may well be TB. He needs a chest x-ray to see if there are any signs of the infection in his lungs.'

A concerned, pleasant, short man with a balding head, wearing a brown suit, he smiled as he looked at me and placed a kind, caring hand on my shoulder. I felt comfortable. Mom clenched her jaw as she looked first at me and then at him.

'Is he going to have to go away to a sanitarium? What about school? What about my other children? What should I tell the neighbors?'

'Let's wait and see what the x-ray shows. If his lungs are clear of infection he won't have to go away, and he won't have to miss school.'

'What's an x-ray mom?' I asked as we left Dr Javett's rooms.

'Let's see if we can find a book to explain what an x-ray is. We can go right now and get a book at the library.' I was thrilled. I had just learned to read at Mrs Barnett's Kindergarten, and I loved the feel of books and the thrill of recognizing words on the pages.

We brought 'The Golden Encyclopedia for Children' home and sat at the dining room table and found the photograph of an x-ray machine.

'That's what we need to do tomorrow, son. They will take a picture of your lungs with a machine like that. Don't tell your father about the x-ray.'

Mom always protected dad from bad news.

The next day she helped me dress in warm clothes with an extra woolen sweater and we took the bus to the radiologist's office on Esselen Street in Hillbrow. A lady in a white uniform led me into a poorly lighted room and showed me where to stand.

'Breathe in,' she commanded.

'Stop breathing.'

There was a faint buzzing sound and then she told me to turn and face the other wall, raise my arms above my head, and she pressed the button again.

'Breathe.'

My father came home from work, he washed his hands in the bathroom next to my room and came in to greet me.

'Hi David. Did you have a good day today?'

I looked at him carefully and nodded my head. I wondered if he could he tell that I had an x-ray? I took the Encyclopedia from under my pillow, where I had hidden it, and showed him the photograph of the x-ray machine and asked him coyly if he knew what it was.

'That's an x-ray machine. Why are you asking?'

'I had one of those today.'

He looked at me quizzically and quickly went looking for my mother. I followed, listening to the discussion from my hiding place in the passage just outside the living room door. Dad wasn't happy that mom hadn't told him about the x-ray.

'What did the x-ray show?'

'I don't know yet. We have to wait until Dr Javett telephones us.'

The doctor called the next day. Apparently, my lungs were clear. Mom told me that most South Africans get TB at some time in their lives, but many could fight the disease without treatment. I could go to school with all the other children without having to worry about anything. We were all relieved, but I was a little disappointed. I liked the special attention as my mother worried about my illness and now that I was alright, she stopped pampering me.

I came down with almost every childhood infectious disease including measles, mumps, German measles, chicken pox, whooping cough, hepatitis, 'strep throat', scarlet fever and 'fevers without name.' In between these episodes I had knee and elbow scrapes, abrasions and minor injuries from playing soccer, cricket, rugby, tennis, table tennis and grass hockey at school and at home.

My mother's ritual when I complained of feeling ill was to feel my face with the back of her hand, and to check my pulse which she had learned while helping the nurses manage South African soldiers wounded during the Second World War. Knowing that she cared and feeling her presence made me feel better.

Her love, empathy and compassion while I suffered through my sore throats, ear aches, chills, rigors, muscle aches, nausea, skin rashes and headaches were so addictive that I sometimes faked illness to get an extra dose. If I told l her I felt sick she took out the glass thermometer from the medicine cabinet and rinsed it under the faucet. I loved to watch her flick the thermometer and shake it to move the mercury down below the red mark before she placed it under my tongue. Three minutes later she removed it from my mouth and I felt like a gladiator in the Circus Maximus waiting for the verdict from the Roman Emperor as she looked at the top of the mercury column– thumbs down I had a fever and my mother frowned, thumbs up my temperature was not elevated, and she is happy. A fever meant she called the doctor and I stayed in bed until my temperature returned to normal.

Mom was concerned, and she loved me. I felt cared for when she said:

'I'll telephone the school. You stay in bed today.'

Most of all I loved the feeling of being tucked securely into bed just after mom lovingly and carefully wiped my face with a warm, slightly moistened flannel face cloth. I loved the soft clean feel of freshly laundered sheets, and pajamas on my skin. She shut the curtains, leaving the room dark as she left me to rest, urging me to sleep, and urged me to call her by ringing the brass bell next to my bed when I awoke.

I read from a collection of comic books, and periodically moved my favorite toy cars on the blankets before wafting off to sleep. Every so often she walked in with a treat: a yummy lunch on a tray, a glass of Coca-Cola with a dollop of vanilla ice cream. Eating this delicious creation made the illness seem much better. The feeling of being loved made me feel good and helped me get well quicker.

Later in the morning our family doctor, Albert Solomon, came to our house to examine me. Dressed in a suit, white shirt, tie and a waistcoat, he carried a heavy leather bag filled with medicine ampoules, syringes, needles, bottles of antiseptic, cotton balls, gauze dressings, tape, a stethoscope, otoscope, flashlight, tongue depressors, a patella hammer and band-aids. He was always kind and gentle. His ritual was always the same and I had a feeling of caring and closeness when he examined my mouth and ears, tapped my chest with his fingers, and listened to my lungs and heart. I got used to his caring and compassion, which contrasted deeply with strict discipline at school. I felt comfort despite my illness. I had the feeling that everything would be fine. I loved the experience of feeling better the next day and getting back to normal.

My mother took me to visit my grandfather at the Johannesburg General Hospital when I was about seven years old. I was struck by the smells of iodine, ether and alcohol as I walked the creaking corridors of linoleum-covered wood floors to his room. I loved seeing the nurses scurrying from bed to bed and seeing them help patients walk to the bathroom. I sensed how the patients felt because I had felt the caring and compassion from my mother and Winnie when I was a patient. It felt so good to have someone care enough about me that they would take time to care for me during my illness, hoping that I would recover my strength. I decided I wanted to be like that. I practiced on my neighbor, Felicity, playing games with a toy stethoscope and a wooden tongue depressor.

During my teenage years my childhood illnesses stopped, and, in their place, I was encouraged to become a 'manly' young man. I drew away from the religion of my youth which taught me humility and concern for my family and neighbors. My school teachers encouraged me to be strong and competitive. The pattern of my education and the strict discipline enabled me to enter medical school at age seventeen.

It would be decades before I remembered what it was that had originally made me want to be a healer.

CHAPTER TWELVE:

༄ஒ

FRIENDSHIP WITH PERKS

W hen I'm scrubbed, wearing a sterile gown and gloves, in the middle of a case in the operating room, a personal telephone call is not only emotionally disruptive, interrupting a complex technical and intellectual exercise, but I can't hold the phone to my ear because that would undo the carefully sterilized space on the patient created to counteract bacterial contamination, which might lead to an infection. If the call is that important the caller will leave a message and I'll call back when I'm done. However, the telephone call this time is directly to the landline in the OR, not to my cell phone, and it is Bill Conway, a pulmonologist, who essentially runs the hospital and has important leadership positions with the Henry Ford Medical Group. He wants to speak to me immediately.

I stop operating and the circulating nurse holds the phone to my ear. A member of the board of trustees has had a breast lump removed by a plastic surgeon in Grosse Pointe, and the pathology shows breast cancer. Can I see him soon? Of course, I can. I'll see him tomorrow morning in my clinic on K8.

Some patients immediately make a big impression, and that is the feeling I have when I shake his hand the next day. Bill Rands, a man about my age, a full head of slightly grey hair, kindly blue eyes, wearing a jacket and tie, alert, and hiding his disbelief and anxiety at the unexpected diagnosis, a man used to being in control, a man whose searing intellect and intelligence enables him to ask probing questions, and to follow each of my answers with more questions, until he is satisfied that he fully understands my opinion. I love patients who ask questions and I love being put on the spot by him. This is one of the reasons I went to medical school and trained in surgical oncology. I want the challenge. I know how to deal with all the questions and the rhetoric that follows.

Male breast cancer is unusual, only approximately twenty-nine hundred cases in the USA per year, compared to at least two hundred and ninety thousand women. Bill tells me he didn't think too much about the lump in his right breast when he saw the plastic surgeon near his home. The doctor removed it through a small incision around the nipple. Bill had received a telephone call a few days later from his primary care physician telling him he had breast cancer. Both men were stunned by the diagnosis because it is so uncommon in men.

The year is 1999. The standard management of male breast cancer is to do a modified radical mastectomy, a technique which has been the guideline approach to male breast cancer for decades, a procedure which includes removing all the breast tissue, including the nipple, and all the lymph nodes in the armpit. I talk and explain and respond and we understand each other well. The scheduling nurse does the paperwork, he signs the consent form and we shake hands.

Bill calls me the next day and he wants to know about a new procedure which he read about. Do I know about this procedure? It is new, and he is not sure if I do the operation, and, if not, he thinks he might want to have his surgery in New York.

In his research Bill had discovered a technique called 'sentinel node biopsy.'

I surprise Bill by explaining that we are part of a North American study, funded by the National Cancer Institute, where we remove the sentinel lymph node, the first lymph node in the armpit to which a breast cancer might spread, a common site of metastasis. If there is tumor in the sentinel node the patient is randomized by a computer in Chicago to either have all the remaining armpit lymph nodes removed or not. The study is designed to determine whether we can avoid removing the rest of the lymph nodes in the axilla, when the sentinel lymph node is positive for tumor, a scientific study which aims to determine whether it is safe to leave the rest of the armpit lymph nodes intact even when there is a small amount of tumor in the node. I'm proud to tell Bill that

I did some of the original research in mice in the 1980s on this concept and, in addition, did the first sentinel node biopsies in patients in Michigan, initially in patients with melanoma and then in patients with breast cancer.

There is one tiny problem with doing a sentinel node biopsy on Bill, rather than removing all his armpit lymph nodes: the study we're doing is for women only, not men. It is also not being done on women outside of the trial since it has not yet been proven to be safe and effective. We are not offering this procedure without patients signing a carefully worded eight-page consent form, which is audited by the NCI.

'I'm so sorry, Mr Rands. The consent states quite clearly that the only patients eligible are women. I can't legally offer this operation to you since you don't fit the required criteria.'

He thinks carefully for a moment. 'How many cases have you done?'

'About three hundred.'

'Well, I think it is quite ok for you to do the operation on me without the approval required for the study. How about if you do it off study? In that way, you don't have to report me as a study case.'

I'm not sure it is bureaucratically safe for me to do this. I know I can do the procedure safely and I feel certain that I'm skilled to accurately find the correct node, an issue that all of us pioneers in this technique have debated for years. Doing an operation 'off protocol' that is basically new and unproven feels a little rebellious and I think carefully about whether I might be reprimanded, or worse, exposed and castigated and advised that I may be obliged to stop operating.

'We should talk about the details of the procedure and, if you still want to chance it, I can do it. Are you sure that this is the direction you want to go?'

'Yes, that's what I'd like to do.'

I explain the techniques that I use, including the part where I inject a blue dye into the breast during the operation while he is under anesthetic. The dye is selectively taken up in the lymphatics that drain the breast tissue, taking fluid from the breast to the sentinel node in the armpit. The dye is absorbed and eventually cleansed from the body through the kidneys. He might pee a bluish, greenish discolored urine for a day or so, a description that raises a smile. We talk for about an hour and he seems content with the plan and our scheduled 'date' in the operating room.

The surgery, removing his right breast and taking out a sentinel lymph node, goes very well. A week later his wound is healing without complications. He has had minimal pain and discomfort.

'The wound looks good and we can take out the drain.' This is a plastic tube which I had left under the skin as a precaution in case he developed fluid in the space where the breast tissue had been removed.

He is anxious to know the result of the pathology review of his tissues.

'The cancer is completely removed with the breast and the margins are clean. The sentinel lymph node did have some tumor in it, and we need to think about what to do with the remaining lymph nodes in your armpit, which we did not remove.'

'What do you normally do in a case like this?'

If he had been a woman with this disease and these findings, we would have removed the remaining armpit lymph nodes, or we would have randomized her on the American College of Surgeons Oncology Group Z0011 study to either having the nodes removed or not. Since he was excluded from this study, I am obliged to tell him that we should probably remove all the remaining nodes.

'Are there disadvantages to removing the remaining lymph nodes?'

'There are potentially three major complications from doing the additional surgery. When we do this surgery, we usually sever a sensory nerve that crosses the armpit and you may feel a little numbness in the upper arm. It involves a small area and usually is tolerated quite well. The skin of the upper arm doesn't have many sensory receptors and the body adapts quite quickly to the point that most people don't notice the sensory loss. Another potential complication of complete axillary lymphadenectomy is lymphedema, or chronic swelling of the arm, which is uncomfortable and incurable, occurring in about twenty percent of patients, requiring massage, compression garments, and physical therapy every day for the rest of your life. The third major complication is limitation of shoulder movement on the side of the surgery, a relatively short-lived problem provided you do vigorous physical therapy at home every day for a few months.'

'What are the advantages of going back to the operating room and removing the remaining lymph nodes?'

'We currently believe that there is a better chance of cure from the cancer. It is probably less likely that the tumor will grow back in the armpit if we remove all the lymph nodes'

'Is it likely that there are more lymph nodes containing tumor in the armpit at this point?'

'The studies show that at least twenty percent of patients with a positive sentinel lymph node will have additional lymph nodes containing tumor in the armpit.'

'Do you think there are other ways of dealing with the remaining tumor in the armpit if it is there?'

'I think you need chemotherapy. This is done under the direction of a medical oncologist. It is possible that chemo could help to control metastases and it is an additional way to offer you a cure from the cancer. You might also need radiation, so I recommend you also consult with a radiation oncologist.'

Bill is a little taken aback by my comments, but it doesn't take him long to move ahead.

'Well, why don't I see the medical oncologist and I'll think a little about what you've said. I'm inclined to skip another operation, but I'll think about it.'

I've already come to understand how courageous he is and how he thinks carefully about everything and I'm quite willing to have him make the decisions that make the most sense to him.

My colleague, doctor Joe Anderson, a medical oncologist, informs me that Bill has decided to take the chemotherapy. I imagine I won't be seeing much of the patient myself, but Bill wants to discuss a few things with me. I suggest we meet for lunch in the Doctor's Dining room on the second floor of the Education and Research Building.

The buffet lunch is a backdrop for a lovely discussion. We discuss all sorts of things and I discover how much Bill loves to think about physics, people, the hospital, and, most importantly, my ideas about how and why tumors grow. I love to talk about these topics and I'm so delighted to have a curious person opposite me, one who delights in my answers and asks appropriate questions. How delightful to share ideas with a person as curious about life as I am. Before we know it, the time has flown by and I need to get back to my clinic. We shake hands and we agree that we should meet again soon.

Three weeks later and we're having lunch again. His hair has begun to thin out from the chemotherapy, but he is tolerating it well. Once again, we easily talk about anything that comes to mind. He has a very deep understanding and interest in tumor growth, and he has spent some time reading and trying to understand my area of research interest, namely, the reasons why tumors spread to other parts of the body.

Our lunch meetings are the highlight of my busy work days. We meet in the Doctor's Dining room almost every month and, one day, when he calls me 'Doctor Nathanson,' I interrupt him and tell him to call me 'David.' He smiles and continues to call me by my professional name and not by my first name.

Months have gone by and Bill has completed his chemotherapy and, after seeing a radiation oncologist, has decided to avoid radiation to the tissues of his chest wall. We're having lunch again and I sense that something is a little different. He is a little pensive when he begins to tell me a story, looking at me over the top of his half-rim glasses, tears welling up in his eyes.

'You remember when you asked me to call you David? I needed to call you by your professional name. I needed to know that you oversaw my case. I needed you to be my doctor. Even though Joe Anderson was responsible for my chemotherapy, I needed to know that you were the chief person in my case, that I could rely on your ideas and opinions. Now I feel like all that has passed, I'm recovered from my surgery and chemotherapy, I feel that everything will be fine, and now I can call you 'David.'

I try to be manly and not cry for this wonderful emotion from a man who I have begun to love like a brother. He has expressed a beautiful feeling of trust, openness and respect, and it is a privilege, one which makes all my work worthwhile. I accept the tenderness in this thought with a gratefulness that I would not have experienced before my learning the true meaning of the word and the emotion from Br David. I feel that Bill is my friend, no longer a patient, like my experience of Marianne when she entrusted me to her inner life, sharing her thoughts and her life with me in emails, letters and cards.

One year after his operation Bill calls me on the telephone.

'David, Happy and I are so grateful for all the excellent treatment I've experienced, and we've talked about how we would like to support one of the programs at Henry Ford Health System. There are a few that seem appropriate to us, but we wondered whether you need any money for your research or clinical programs?'

I hesitate for only a moment. It is difficult to find funding from the NCI or other funding organizations, particularly for a surgeon who is not doing research full time, and I would love to have a source of funding that would allow me to continue doing the clinical and translational research that I've been doing for decades, spending months out of every year writing grant proposals, repeatedly rejected by scientific committees, often by serious scientists who may not truly understand my hypotheses and intentions.

'Bill, I think you, Happy and I should meet to discuss this in some detail. I'll write a proposal and explain what my intentions are.'

'Ok. Let's do that. I'll set up a dinner at our club in Grosse Pointe and we'll talk about the details. Just email me a list of optional dates and we'll be there together.'

The dinner is lovely. Bill's wife Happy certainly fits her name. Their story is quite unique. It seems they are both orphans, adopted by loving couples, and grew up within a few blocks of each other, attending the same schools, but didn't meet until they were both young adults in college. Bill went to Yale, and Happy was at school on the East coast; they came back to Detroit. They married and had children and Bill spent many years in the banking profession while Happy was a cheery housewife, living in a beautiful house, in a gorgeous neighborhood, near Lake St Claire, with lots of friends and acquaintances in the Detroit area and far beyond. Bill left banking and has his own investment business.

I show Bill and Happy my proposal after dinner, sitting in the genteel atmosphere of their club, content and open to ideas and discussion. I tell them the background of funded 'chairs' at Henry Ford Health System. Many grateful patients have donated money to fund 'chairs' in different departments. The 'chairs' cost one million dollars apiece. Recipients of the funds can use about four to five percent of the money annually.

'A good way for us to advance breast cancer knowledge and the management of the disease is to fund a Breast Cancer Research Chair.'

I have drawn a few diagrams, and an outline of potential directions that we could focus on at Henry Ford. Both Bill and Happy ask a lot of questions and they seem really enthralled with the idea. Bill has an astute business brain and he wants to speak to senior administration at Henry Ford. He believes that we need a commitment from the leaders that they will match the funds and make sure that the money doesn't disappear down some mysterious hole in the administration. He shares his concern about this, but he will make sure that he gets to speak to the leaders himself.

I know nothing about the various ways that donated money is distributed and I'm quite happy to have Bill spin his magical personality with the important people in the institution. Over the next few months he comes up with a plan that includes he and Happy donating a half-million dollars to start the process. The rest will come from other donors and we manage to persuade a group of charitable women who have raised money for a chair in Palliative Medicine to work on ways to do the same for Bill and Happy's chair. The women are lovely to work with and they organize annual dinners at the Detroit Athletic club to raise money. It takes six years and, finally, we have enough money to create the 'chair.'

The leaders choose me to be the recipient of the chair, a great honor and I am delighted to receive the award at a banquet at the Townsend Hotel in Birmingham, Michigan in April 2007. There are tributes and speeches galore, including lovely flattering and kind words from Nancy Schlichting, Chief Executive Officer of the HFHS, and from Mark Kelley, chairman of the Henry Ford Medical Group. I've invited my mentor, Don Morton, to be my guest and I'm very emotional and choked up when I stand at the podium and tell the audience how influential he has been in my career, how he taught me so many wonderful ways to manage complex cancer cases, how he has influenced the management of many thousands of patients by his direct intervention when they sought his opinion in his clinic, and also because he has trained almost one hundred surgical oncologists, like me, who practice all over the country, treating cancer patients; every time those patients are treated, Don Morton's influence is there in the imagination of those surgeons. He is moved and gives a short speech, telling anecdotes about me to the audience of seventy people. Some of his stories elicit laughter from my friends in the audience. I'm touched when he tells everyone about my mouse experiments in the 1980s and how they influenced him in his development of sentinel lymph node biopsy for melanoma patients.

I can now use the money from the Rands Chair for studies and continue collecting data from every breast cancer patient who has undergone a sentinel node biopsy. This requires an expert abstractor and I find Patricia Baker in the department of Biostatistics and Research Epidemiology. I had started collecting the data in 1995, using other sources of money, but now I have enough money to up the rate of collection. Keeping a data base is an expensive undertaking and could result in important findings that might even change the way we practice.

A little appreciated advantage of having extra money in an institution like Henry Ford is that I can now support the careers of carefully selected residents and medical students in training by offering them an opportunity to do research with me. I had already done this with several residents, none of whom ended up in academic practice, but did find ways to excel in their surgical careers in other ways.

I do manage to interest David Kwon to change his plans and to follow in my footsteps in a career in Surgical Oncology. After working with me as a second-year resident he decides he wants to do a fellowship in Surgical Oncology. He works diligently and, after a carefully placed telephone call to my friend, chief of surgery at MD Anderson Cancer Center in Houston, possibly the best training hospital in the world for this discipline, David is accepted as a two-year fellow, returning to HFHS as a senior staff person who advances rapidly to become chief of Surgical Oncology and in a leadership position for the new Henry Ford Cancer Center, the new building scheduled to open in 2020.

Four other trainees whose careers moved into surgical oncology because of my influence are Terry Sarantou, who landed a fellowship with Don Morton in Los Angeles and now directs the prestigious American College of Surgeons National Accreditation Program for Breast Centers; Rupen Shah, who completed his residency at HFHS and did a two year fellowship at Roswell Park Cancer Institute in Buffalo and then came back to join us as a fully trained and board certified surgical oncologist; Kelly Rosso who did a breast fellowship at MD Anderson Cancer Center and is now in practice in Phoenix; Clara Park who also did a breast fellowship at MD Anderson and is now on the faculty at Ohio State University doing research and taking care of patients with breast diseases.

The other remarkable spin-off from the Rands Chair comes from the Team Angels, a group of mostly Italian women who live in Macomb County. Rosalba Pacella started this group of philanthropically-minded women after her brother died of breast cancer in his late forties. She and he were very close siblings and she was devastated by the way the lump in his breast, ignored initially by the patient, was also apparently brushed off by his doctor until it grew to a size when treatment was essential, but too late to save his life. Rosalba was determined that the public should become aware of the possibility of men getting breast cancer.

Rosalba approached our Philanthropy Department at HFHS hoping they would steer her Team Angels to professionals taking care of patients with breast cancer. The neat part of this story is that the philanthropy professionals quickly realized that Rosalba's committee knew they could give their money to different institutions, so we had to come up with an idea that would influence them to choose us. The obvious connection was the focus on breast cancer in men. Who better to show our commitment to men with breast cancer than Bill Rands?

The Team Angels organization rallied around an angel symbol because of Rosalba's experience with an angel. She describes this in my book on Breast Cancer survivors published in 2007. Her committee took the usual symbol for breast cancer, a pink ribbon in a sort of alpha arrangement and added a thin layer of blue along the edge to represent men. The angel is in the middle where the ribbon crosses over itself.

Rosalba and her treasurer met Bill and me and a representative from the philanthropy office for lunch in the Doctor's Dining room. Bill's friendly, welcoming personality, and my presentation of our program won them over and they committed to send us money every year.

I have included brief anecdotes and stories in this discussion because the people I have described are all extremely caring individuals. What connects all the people in this chapter is their 'giving' attitudes. They all care about others in a deep way or they wouldn't be able to devote their time to other people. The doctors are devoted to patient care and they spend every day going above and beyond what would constitute an ordinary day of work. They have committed their lives to the management of patients and their problems. Bill and Happy, whose personalities glow with warmth and caring for others, continue to share their lives with us, to the extent that Bill sometimes gets calls from people with newly diagnosed breast cancer and he has on more than one occasion jumped into his car and driven to a stranger's house to provide a caring hand because a new diagnosis of breast cancer is so devastating to the patient. He has been there, and he is quite comfortable sharing his experiences. Rosalba and her 'girls' may have an advantage in the emotional 'department' because of their Mediterranean origins. I'm pretty sure that there is a familial, and probably a genetic reason why they are so giving and so warm, sharing their emotions and their extra-ordinary cooking with all of us, caring for the underdog, the sick, and anyone who needs a loving hug.

My own ability to care deeply did not suddenly appear after my experiences at Esalen and with Br David and Francis Lu. I grew up in a caring environment, promoted by my grandmother, my parents, my religious education with Mr Kahn, the time spent as a Boy Scout, my exposure to the humanities in High School, being in the presence of great teachers in medical school, and a deep involvement in the world of classical music with my friend Melvyn, starting at a very young age.

There's a part of us as physicians that explodes with empathy for patients and their families. Somehow, we sense or feel what they experience when stricken with an illness. We see many examples of suffering and we encounter this at a relatively early age; as medical students and then throughout our years of training and then as practitioners of the art and science of Medicine.

I had seen thousands of women with breast diseases, some of them with cancer, too many of them. It was obviously important for me to know many of the details of diagnosis and clinical management of breast conditions, particularly in a rapidly evolving world of technology, surgical techniques, radiology, molecular biology, immunology and pharmacogenetics. But, as a trained observer, I noticed something else amongst my predominantly female patients: they needed something different than their husbands and sons, or boyfriends. They didn't complain directly but I immersed myself in asking them the question:

'Are you comfortable getting your clinical breast care in the hospital, sharing clinic waiting space with trauma, vascular and general surgery patients?'

Many women said it was fine. But many said they would prefer to be in a clinic designed for women, away from men patients. They even said they would prefer a separate entrance into the medical facility.

Breast centers were popping up all over the country, mostly free-standing facilities funded by surgeons in private practice. My site visit at the Cleveland clinic in 2001 sparked an idea that we should develop Multidisciplinary Breast Diagnostic Clinics at HFH. I used my skills in grant writing to imagine and plan for organizing MBDCs throughout the Ford facilities: at the main hospital downtown, and the other HFHS facilities throughout

South-East Michigan -West Bloomfield, Lakeside and Fairlane. There were two major hurdles: money and space.

Several administrators were not enthusiastic and discouraged me from doing this. But I was determined to forge ahead and that was when the ideas for a new West Bloomfield Hospital started to emerge from the CEO of HFHS, Nancy Schlichting. A major new hospital, built from the ground up, at the suburban medical center where I had been operating and doing clinics since 1987. That would be the best place to build a new Breast Center, where breast surgeons and breast imaging radiologists could work side-by-side. Where could I get the money to build this Center?

The Office of Philanthropy suggested that we approach Benson Ford and his sister. Over lunch one day I presented my ideas to them. The next day Benson gave us a sizeable check. Not enough to build the Breast Center, but certainly a substantial start. Jeannie Maxbauer, my Philanthropy liaison, came up with the idea of an annual fund-raising luncheon for Mothers, Daughters, Sisters, and Friends of breast cancer patients, who were also at risk for getting the disease themselves. These highly successful events helped us raise $2.8 million, enough to fund the 8800-square foot facility. After many hours of meetings with architects, administrators, breast radiologists, nurses and interior design experts, the facility was built on the second floor of the West Clinic building at the West Bloomfield Hospital. We opened our doors within a month of the opening of the new hospital.

How do we evaluate the success of this caring adventure? Perhaps by looking at the number of patients who we treat with breast cancer now compared to eight years ago – that has more than tripled to about 360 patients per year. The number of breast imaging procedures, including mammograms, ultrasounds and breast biopsies, has more than doubled in the last eight years. The facility is beautiful, thanks to many caring people and all started by Francee and Benson Ford, whose name sits above the entrance.

I never imagined being a breast surgeon, or to be working in a breast center where I interact with breast radiologists every day. And, to cap it all, I can fully express my empathy for the many women patients who have breast cancer treated by our team.

CHAPTER THIRTEEN:

∽◌∾

GRATEFULNESS

I'm walking in San Francisco on a Sunday morning in October 1995. The Commission on Cancer meeting starts this afternoon and I have a few hours to kill.

It's 10.45 am and I cross California Street on the corner of Grant Avenue. The placard on the sidewalk outside Old Saint Mary's Church, built in 1853 and rebuilt after the 1906 earthquake, advertises an 11.00 am talk by Brother David Steindl-Rast entitled; 'Christianity and Buddhism.' I feel that I'm somehow meant to be here. The title talks to me. Something uncanny about this active parish of the archdiocese, serving the Chinatown and Nob Hill communities of San Francisco, invites me inside.

The church basement is filled with rows of fold-up chairs and a simple wooden podium up front. A few people are sitting, and some are filling cups with coffee at the back of the room. I sit in the front row. I've been reading Christian theology recently, trying hard to understand the religion and its history. I know very little about Buddhism. The title of the talk is confusing to me. Why would someone be talking about two traditions that seem to teach different messages? And who is this person giving the talk?

Brother David, wearing a simple, clean, white, turtle neck cotton shirt, a simple black sleeveless waistcoat, khaki pants, comfortable brown leather sandals, a mischievous twinkle in his eye, bushy eyebrows dominating his face, a warm smile expanding into the gentle stubble of a trimmed beard, walks into the room and to the podium. His thinning grey hair blends into a forehead of gentle wrinkles, while he unconsciously plays with an old partial amputation of one of his fingers, strumming aimlessly across the foreshortened tip with his thumb, prayer beads hanging from his left hand, a bright expression of pure love, he exudes a saintly aura.

After a brief introduction by a church member, the pious Benedictine from the Calmodulese Monastery in Big Sur greets the audience. His first words are simple, direct and pierce my heart and soul.

'Christianity is the tradition of the Word and Buddhism is the tradition of silence. Without the silence one cannot hear the Word.'

Stunningly meaningful, yet so simple on the surface, the concept surprises and amazes me.

He tells us that Buddhist teachings encourage the practice of 'deep' listening. Silence, turning away from noise and distraction, encourages us to pay attention, and to embrace quiet, alone in a positive way, in a way that endorses dynamic tranquility. The heartfelt Christian humbly trusts in God, while the silence includes an emptying of the mind to receive wisdom, insight, and understanding. In this way one may joyously discover a new, interior freedom that will make one feel more vibrant, more fully alive, more mindful and grateful.

The monastic traditions, both East and West, cultivate mindfulness, a term much misused because it perhaps sounds like mind-over-body, but has nothing to do with mind over or against body. 'Wholeheartedness' is the English word that Br David prefers, that you respond to every situation from the heart, that you listen with your heart to every situation, and your heart elicits a response.

The experience of a new understanding, whatever the topic, is always so meaningful to me. Five years after my transformative encounter at Esalen, searching for 'truth,' experiencing the world through my work as a surgeon-scientist, the humble tranquility of the church basement, and the softly-spoken words of a modern Christian sage with Buddhist proficiency, enlightens me and urges me to discover further encounters with Br David.

My first Esalen experience with Brother David is a five-day workshop entitled 'Poetry East and West,' where I discover something deep inside me that I believe has always been there, suppressed by my monomaniacal scientific and clinical endeavors. The soft underbelly of my deep soul, the poetry hidden for so long, dying to emerge and enlighten me and others, bursts forth, a volcanic eruption spewing years of pent up wisdom, like larva, contained in a deep cavern, boiling and blowing off the top of a mountain, the poems, like tons of magma, shooting into the vacant space towards the sky, covering the landscape and the people with a dream-like element, many years of hidden knowledge suddenly free to roam and express.

In addition to a PhD in Experimental Psychology from the University of Vienna, monastic training in Upstate New York, and a stint at a Buddhist Monastery, Br David had spent time studying poetry and literature at Columbia University in New York. He had been the scholar in residence at the Esalen Institute in Big Sur. He radiates wisdom and a beautiful love of nature, words, animals and people.

Like many others before me, I feel drawn to Brother David because of the calm, pious, graceful, grateful and loving wisdom that he exudes whenever he enters a space with other people present. I soon learn that he and Francis Lu, a psychiatrist from San Francisco, run a five- day film workshop at Esalen, one so popular that it is difficult to obtain a place.

Francis and Br David had met at Esalen in 1989 and developed an immediate connection when they talked about film as a vehicle for spiritual experiences and development. Francis noted how movies could facilitate contemplation and Br David had experienced how film had assisted monks in meditation. The two planned and held their first co-led film seminar, 'Film and contemplation,' in 1990. Both, deeply moved by the discussions and the seminar attendees' personal experiences of the films, continued to work together and, learning from each other, joined each summer at Esalen by people from many different walks of life, they continued to select spiritual themes every year, expanding the workshop to seven days. They selected movies that illustrated themes that touched the soul and were also considered artistic masterpieces. The movies often depicted characters who experienced an epiphany that led to a transformation of consciousness, especially powerful when shown in the contemplative setting of Esalen, 'undistracted by the everyday world, senses opened and sharpened by the Pacific Ocean.'

The spiritual theme in 2002 is gratefulness and, having read Br David's books, I decide this workshop is perfect for me. The catalogue description for the seminar identifies gratefulness as the key to joy, the pathway to happiness. Before selecting the movies, Br David and Francis have done extensive research, and discussed in what sequence they should be shown.

I'm so familiar with Esalen that it is like going home for me and, on Sunday night, entering the room called 'Huxley' in the main building, a large, green-carpeted room, sparsely furnished, a large movie screen suspended from the ceiling, home theater equipment connected by a vast array of wires, I settle into a plastic chair with twenty-nine other movie lovers in chairs or on floor pillows.

Francis announces the 'rules of the house,' meant to honor the intention of silence and contemplation, and quite different from attending movies in theaters back home in Michigan. The ritual of movie watching at every session consists of entering the room quietly, not talking to fellow seminarians, sitting comfortably, settling into silence and the darkness as the lights are dimmed and the movie is projected onto the screen. I have a pen and a journal, ready to write my experiences. I'm primed to look carefully at anything in the movie that strikes me as exemplifying the theme of gratitude, maybe a character's story, or a facial expression, or a beautiful landscape, or a musical theme, or an animal, or something completely unexpected.

At the film's conclusion, we sit in silence for a few minutes with the lights off, and, for the next five minutes, I sit and think about scenes that had the most effect on me, looking at the notes I've made in the dark, reliving those experiences, making additional notes, and moving my chair into the circle of seminarians to talk about their experience. Francis tells us what scene affected him the most, and the microphone is passed sequentially clockwise from one person to the next, each of us given about one minute to identify one scene or image that moved us. Some want to keep talking about multiple scenes, some want to express their own philosophies, and I want to be unique in what I experienced, finding that a few others saw scenes or images in almost the same way as I have done. Each time someone describes a scene I relive it in my mind, further enriching my appreciation of the film while giving me additional insights into the ideas and personality of every workshop participant.

Br David contributes his favorite scene and, every time he talks, I realize that he loves animals (particularly cats), and he sees the world through loving eyes, always grateful for things that I just take for granted. At the end of every evening session, we stand in a circle, holding hands, as Br David expresses his gratefulness to the people that helped him get safely to Esalen, the airline pilots, the security agents at the airports, the taxi drivers; or the people that enhance his stay, like the gardeners who grow our food, the farmers who tend the coffee beans, the people who clean the rooms; or the people who fill in for him at the monastery while he's away: and the ocean that washes on the shore below, the sealions that bark at night from the coastline, the Monarch butterflies resting in the trees on their long migration, and a lot more. Each day, hearing him say such warm, kind things about everything, I feel closer to nature and my fellow humans, putting aside my natural tendency to look critically at the complex sides of life, perpetually needing to solve problems. Each day I feel more grateful, and privileged, and I imagine behaving differently with my patients, and with the people back home that I live and work with.

Br David and Francis have written about and discussed what gratitude does for each of us, and they believe that it is just as important for others that we encounter in our daily lives, because it calms our fears, strengthens our courage, opens our hearts for adventure, and is more than likely to heal us. When we feel these positive feelings, we are more likely to permeate love and contentment into our environment, which will likely be sensed by the people we encounter, and they are often likely to respond in kind.

The films in the workshop are connected to each other, reflecting themes of the gratefulness of family members for each other; younger or less fortunate people for older, wiser and compassionate characters who reciprocate love; the gratitude amongst complete strangers caught in unusual circumstances; and the gratefulness of students for mentors. Every one of these themes resonates with me as I remember images from my own childhood, adolescence, early manhood, and my recent adult self.

One movie stands out: 'Tuesdays with Morrie,' a movie, based on Mitch Albom's best-selling memoir about his real-life trips to his former college professor at Brandeis University, Morrie Schwartz, who is dying of Lou Gehrig's disease (ALS), that shows Mitch's growing awareness and increasing gratitude for his mentor. I have read the book, heard him interviewed on the radio, and I had seen the movie in the theater near my house in Michigan. But, seeing it again at the film workshop, in a tranquil setting, close to the blue sea, sky, trees, gardens, new friends, with Francis and Br David, I'm digesting and feeling Mitch, journalist, radio host, sports aficionado from Detroit, my adopted home, in a new way, as he develops a deepening gratefulness for Morrie's insights. I see myself in him as he visits Morrie and comes to understand the importance of living meaningfully every day in the face of death.

In Morrie I remember with heightened gratefulness all my important mentors, the people who influenced me the most, who affected the person I have become;

Mrs Barnett, my kindergarten teacher, who taught me how to love reading; Bill Lamont and the beginnings of my 'manliness' in elementary school; Herman Kahn, a German Holocaust survivor, my religion teacher in elementary school, who taught me the Bible and showed me how to honor the Sabbath, to revere my family and friends, and to be kind and compassionate; Jan Hoffmeier, my high school mathematics teacher who trained me to draw perfect circles in geometry, and think through algebra and trigonometry, giving me a way to see the world of disciplined carefulness; Dan Henning, my senior high school geography teacher, who gently coaxed me into a life in medicine; my English teacher, Buck Rodgers, who instilled a love of words, sentences and stories; Philip Tobias, chairman of the Anatomy Department at Wits medical school, principle of the University, three times on a short list for a Nobel prize, my teacher and mentor in Medical School, who enabled me to experience his great wisdom and enthusiasm for anatomy, paleoanthropology, the inquiry into the unknown, and the evolution of Man; Daniel DuPlessis, chairman of surgery in Johannesburg, who taught me how to be a high-quality surgeon and to dedicate my life to my patients; Bert Myberg, Rhodes scholar, athlete, innovative surgeon, who started the organ transplant division at the Johannesburg General Hospital in my first post-graduate year, and who inspired me to do a fellowship in immunology; John Fahey, chairman of the Department of Microbiology and Immunology at UCLA, discoverer of immunoglobulin D, who admitted me, a foreign medical graduate, to his department as a fellow in 1975, giving me the opportunity to grow, flourish and create a new mindset, introducing me to my other self, the inquiring scientist; Don Morton, chief of Surgical Oncology at UCLA, whose approach to cancer included intense interest in laboratory investigations that would eventually lead to the important regrowth of immunotherapy in the successful treatment of many cancers, and his unique clinical approaches to the effective multidisciplinary management of complex cancer cases; Bill Blaisdell, chairman of surgery at UC Davis, an energetic surgeon who enhanced my surgical skills; and other great teachers that influenced me.

Seeing the movie brings forth memories of these great mentors, unleashing an intense feeling of gratefulness to their impact on my life.

In the movie Morrie appears happy, vigorous, witty, courageous, and wise, despite his increasing weakness and his dependence upon others to survive, giving Mitch ideas, instructions and advice. Mitch, leading a pressured life, with scant room for appreciating meaningful relationships, becomes more understanding of his girlfriend and the crazy life he leads, which requires him to travel, meet deadlines, be out late, eat on the run, and generally lead a frenetic life, like many people I know, including me. Morrie is the sage, bringing spiritual wisdom and a sense of the divine in the face of his own mortality, and, in his dying, I feel my own sadness at losing my teachers. Perhaps this is a wake-up call for me, like it was for Mitch. I think it is time for me to re-evaluate my own lifestyle and my approach to patients, nurses, students, and my own family. It is time to learn to enjoy those things that I have, and to be grateful every day of my life. This is my epiphany.

Looking around at the workshop participants and speaking to them at mealtimes, it seems that everyone has had their own individual epiphany of remembered love, caring, friendships, mentorships, sharing their experiences in an open, awe-inspiring, trusting and friendly way which I feel in an increasingly palpable manner. Br David brings his own reassuring presence and keen intelligence about gratefulness, his delight and joy at seeing the film images, his constant encouragement to stay in the present moment, urging us to process together the spiritual meanings of our combined experience.

Almost everyone in the workshop wants to speak to Br David. I want to spend time alone with him and I'm not sure how to ask him for that privilege. He always has someone with him, and he doesn't seem to have any time for a one-on-one. I occasionally sit with him at mealtime in the dining room, but there are always people around, and the situation seems non-conducive to the types of questions I have for him, deep issues that I live with and think about almost every day. Then I experience a miracle.

I'm sitting at the end of one of the long wooden lunch tables and Br David is sitting at the other end, not within easy distance to even have a simple conversation without shouting. On each side of the rectangular table are six workshop participants, enjoying their lunch and talking to each other. There's a lively conversation at Br David's end of the table, and I catch only the occasional sentence, while I indulge in my own conversations at my end of the table. I look at Br David periodically, hoping that there will be a lull in his encounter, so I can get up and walk over to him and ask if I can talk to him privately. He stands, and one of the women asks him if she can walk with him around the grounds this afternoon, and he raises his voice just a little, looks straight at me and says: 'I can't do that today. I have an appointment with David.'

Stunned, I walk over to him, and he smiles at me, a twinkle in his eye, and he asks, politely and gently, if I'm still available for a walk past the art barn and the school.

Walking toward the garden he starts by asking me what I've been doing since we last met, and he remembers that I have done some prior workshops with him, and that I was at St Mary's in San Francisco, an astute memory for anyone, particularly for a monk who travels extensively and probably meets thousands of people every year. He observes beautiful flowers with a child-like excitement, and points out the small Buddha garden statue to the left of the path, and then we follow the path across the narrow wooden bridge that connects the two sides of the property, crossing over a stream and waterfall that comes from the mountains inland, past the circular meditation hut, the small parking lot, and the steep road heading towards the Yurt on the left and the tiny school yard on the right for the children of residents of the area, the other pathway heading left toward the sea, the Big House on the edge of the cliff, built by Dr Murphy in the early twentieth century.

By now I am well into my questions for the great thinker, which he deals with carefully, thoughtfully and fully. I want to know about his spiritual practice and his frequent reference to the importance of rediscovering the child within us. He tells me that monks like him are fortunate to live in an environment where deep, contemplative thought is possible, but he believes that this is something that I can do even though I don't live in a monastery. The trick is to be mind-full, and he spells out the word to show me that the accent is on the words 'fullness, wholeness or wholeheartedness.'

'The full view is to see each situation as purely 'gratis,' or 'free,' and, if you do that, your response is 'gratefulness.' That is simply it. That is my practice. I try to live gratefully. That is not the same as saying 'thank you' when you are given something, even something materially valuable, by someone. What I mean by being grateful puts the accent on 'fullness.' That happens when you experience the gift within you. We have hundreds of opportunities every day to be grateful, to feel joy. We may take for granted that we have our first cup of coffee in the morning, and, if we think about how that coffee got to our cup, and we are grateful for the farmer who spends his life growing the beans, and stores them, transports them to the nearest port, how the ship carries the bags of beans to a port, one can be grateful to all the people involved in this process without even knowing them personally. If you slept well last night, think about those who are insomniacs, and you can learn to think about those that are not as fortunate as you are, you who can see while others are blind, or others who cannot walk, or some who are sick in bed, or dying. Even before you start thinking of those other people not as fortunate as you, it is a good thing to enjoy what you have. There is opportunity upon opportunity to be grateful. That's what life is.'

These ideas resonate strongly with me because they remind me of my childhood in South Africa, particularly my exposure to my first Hebrew teacher, Herman Kahn, in Yeoville, Johannesburg, at the Adat Yeshurun congregation, a survivor of unspeakable hardship during the Nazi times in Germany, who taught me to be respectful of my elders, and to the Torah, the Five Books of Moses. I had felt the same joy and respect for my teachers and mentors when I grew up, and when I went to medical school, feeling a true sense of reverence towards my anatomy school cadaver and to the many patients I met during my training.

But now, listening and feeling Br David's words, I realize that surgical training, both in South Africa and in the United States, had likely stripped away the natural feelings of awe, joy and wonder that I had earlier in my life. The hard lifestyle of the surgeon, accompanied by inconsistent and uncontrollable sleep patterns, personally derogatory behaviors from my teachers, a hefty load of extremely sick patients, each one needing my alert attention, gut-wrenching losses, inadequate time and space to mentally process family dramas (my own and those of my patients), dealing with death in a perfunctory way, like soldiers in a war zone losing their buddies, is clearly evident to me walking next to Br David who had not dealt with trauma and drama like I had.

'If you train yourself to be grateful for everything, every moment, you still have to deal with things you don't like.'

It's almost as if he is reading my mind as I tell him about the difficult life of a surgeon.

'One can train oneself to be grateful for everything, all the time, at every moment of every day. You will take the opportunity to be alert to the gift within every gift, even when you are obliged to deal with those things you don't like, because you will take the opportunity to do something about it.'

It's so easy to talk to him and his responses seem so fluid, so dynamic, so sensible, an expert in the topic that he has promoted, studied, and embedded himself in for years. I wonder what I would say if he asked me how I know how to remove a tumor from the stomach, or the colon, or any other organ. There are certain technical aspects that I could describe to him, but he would need to know detailed anatomy, physiology and pathology for him to understand me fully. So, I ask my next question with a little trepidation, realizing that I cannot fully understand how he practices 'wholeheartedness' in the moment without knowing the ideas and information he lives with every day, his knowledge of Jesus and the Gospels, for example, or perhaps his knowledge of St Benedict.

'How do you practice 'wholeheartedness?

'I try to be present to what confronts me wherever I am. Right now, I'm practicing enjoying your company and answering your questions, thinking about how you might feel when you ask for answers about where you are in your profession, and in your deep feelings about God. This is quite simple, and we tend to forget how many hours each day we already spend with living our lives simply walking, like we are doing now, and how we could enjoy the very process of walking. I enjoy just feeling my feet on the earth. The same could apply to you when you drive your car to work every day, pushing your foot down on the gas pedal or feeling your foot on the break as you slow down. It's as simple as that. Children do this all the time, and this is one of the reasons why I encourage people to be again like they were as children.'

My questions and conflicts relate to my scientific education, my need to answer everything in this world with scientific certainty, based entirely upon scientific experiments, designed to address the subjects that I deal with every day of my life. I read scientific articles in prestigious journals based upon the biology of a disease and, in my case, I focus heavily upon why cancer spreads to lymph nodes. Br David can't answer those questions for me, and I realize that talking to him brings out issues that I think about outside of my scientist's mind.

How can I rediscover the child within me while dealing with disease, suffering, a world of cynicism and loss of civility, and death?

'I would say that we all seek to find meaning in life. That's what we do when we're adults, and we strive to understand why we're even here, why we even are living. As children we are just happy to be, to play with our friends, to taste the ice cream, wanting another spoonful, running on the sandy beach, feeling the surf on our feet, playing board games with the neighbor, eating our favorite cookie, swimming on a warm summer day, even returning to school after summer vacation, excited to see our friends again. We have done that as children, and we can do it as adults if we try.'

I'm not sure he really understands what it's like to be in my position when I operate on patients, or wrestle with the angel of death, but his genuine enthusiasm feels so good as I look at him energetically climbing the hill towards Highway One. From that vantage point we look back at the ocean, the tall trees, the mowed grass, and the mountains rising out of the sea, a tranquil scene, unchanged from prior years while the world reels from mounting terrorism.

On the way back to the main building I struggle with the idea of bringing up the topic of spiritual faith, a subject which has haunted me since my first epiphany at Esalen twelve years ago. My knowledge of Christianity is so tiny next to his that I'm reluctant to expose how little I know. Perhaps I can ask him a few things, tell him what I've been doing with my reading of Christianity, and see where we go. I tell him a little and ask him what he would recommend I read to help me understand why I don't understand how Jesus can be my savior.

'What you're feeling is a sense of yearning and, as soon as you come to terms with that, as soon as you realize that, you will know that is the direction where God lies.'

I've never heard him refer to God directly because he has always been respectful of my Jewish background. In other workshops, even a weekend workshop on 'The living Bible,' with workshop attendees from different faiths, he often uses a term such as 'the all-powerful,' or 'the One.' I had stopped going to synagogue at age fifteen when my rabbi failed to acknowledge my question about the age of the universe, a subject where scientific evidence showed billions of years and yet the rabbi insisted on talking about six thousand years, the typical biblical exegesis. Now I'm urgently looking for God, not knowing where to go, and afraid to ask Br David directly, expecting that he would answer me like my rabbi, making me lose my faith in his piety and wisdom.

'Where is God and how does He relate to gratefulness?' I ask.

'The simplest common denominator in all religious traditions is which way to go to find meaning in life. I'm a Christian but my great grandfather was Jewish, a wealthy Jew from a medium size town in Austria. Everyone has religious experiences, whether they are in some way associated with organized religion. A Christian is a person whose spiritual quest in some way or another has received a decisive impetus through Jesus. I would say that whenever you find meaning in life you are having a religious experience, because the religion within all religions is the quest for meaning. Your yearning for God is your religion, whatever you call it. An organized religion like Judaism, or Christianity or Islam is not automatically religious; you must make it religious, your religion, by linking it with your own experience, tying it back to your own experience of meaningful living. When you experience moments of insight, you're having what Maslow called a 'peak,' or 'mystical' experience. We might call this experiencing communion with ultimate reality. And this is akin to feeling profound gratefulness.'

In my tradition, which I thoroughly believed and lived daily until my teenage years, I whispered a prayer as soon as I woke up in the morning and savored the vitality of sleep. I thanked God for allowing me to see and to pee, to eat and to walk, to dress and to have clothes to wear, to have my mother and father love me, and to feel safe when I walked to school. Biblical stories, filled with legends, wars, mystical miracles, heroes and kings, were lovely to read but I always had a concern that God could get so angry that He could send plagues, floods, and terrible evil to destroy us if we weren't good, obeying the Commandments, showing our reverence in the synagogue, being kind to each other and to strangers. Here I'm on an afternoon stroll with a man of God, who is telling me something quite similar without the angry part, telling me that I can live wholeheartedly, that I can rejuvenate myself by all the good things that come out of being grateful, or, as I found in a David Whyte poem: 'To be human is to become visible while carrying what is hidden as a gift to others.'

Profoundly affected by my week of open emotions, sharing feelings with others, experiencing the humble gratefulness of Br David and the others in the film workshop, I return to my busy surgical practice in Detroit, ready to turn my surgical personality upside down. This is a little scary for someone who believed so fully in the need to be tough to succeed in my profession. For the first time in my life I'm ready to show my newfound humility to patients, students, surgical trainees, my colleagues, friends and family. I feel like I belong to everyone and everyone belongs to me. How will I continue to excel in my profession within a new frame of mind?

CHAPTER FOURTEEN:

༄ⲷⲷⲷ

RESPECT FOR THE DEAD

I t is a warm sunny summer day in January 1962 and I'm about to meet my first
cadaver. I breathe deeply and enter the venerable University of the Witwatersrand (Wits) Medical School, a three-story, rectangular building. The foundation
stone for the medical school on Hospital Hill had been laid by the Governor
General of South Africa, Viscount Buxton, in January 1920. The elegant old
structure has a lower ground floor, a ground floor and a first floor and an inner
courtyard and garden, built on the slope of Hospital Hill, across the street from
the Johannesburg General Hospital. The detail in the brickwork, the design of
the staircases, the woodwork of the doors and arched window frames, the precise
masonry on the granite stone courses and cement corner finishes, the brass door
handles, the wrought iron lamp fittings, and the visually dominant guardrail covering the parapet on the ground and first floors on the east elevation, all show
beautiful craftsmanship. The Harveian lecture theater is the main assembly hall,
a revered space that has supported the education of thousands of medical, dental,
physical and occupational therapy students since its opening in 1928.

This is my first day in the anatomy dissection hall. I feel my heart pound-
ing in my chest. Will I be up to the rigors of a medical education?

My crisp new white laboratory coat makes me feel professional. I belong
here. I know it. I make my way towards the Vesalian Dissection Hall, named

after Andreas Vesalius, sixteenth century founder of modern human anatomy. Despite my attempt to look nonchalant in front of my medical school classmates, I keep recalling the stories I'd heard of medical students fainting when first entering the anatomy dissection hall. Would I be one of those? I had never seen a cadaver. Not even my grandfather who died when I was eleven.

Like rats lured by the Pied Piper, the new students follow each other down an old, wide, long corridor with a linoleum-lined floor, the walls on both sides completely covered from floor to ceiling by death masks, made by placing wet plaster over the face of a recently deceased person and, upon solidifying, the face reconstructed from a mold of the cast, and completed by artists who painted the features to make them more vivid. I feel this is my introduction to the cadavers I'm about to see and, being a child of Apartheid South Africa, raised in a country run by a minority White government intolerant of 'lesser racial groups,' a wake-up call to introduce me to the multicultural society which I have chosen to serve. There are sections devoted to the different racial groups, chosen from a collection of ten thousand such masks, housed and maintained in the anatomy department.

All the faces mounted on the corridor walls are varied, a protean collection of facial features with an array of unique brows, eyes, skin colors, noses, lips, teeth and jaws collected by the anatomy staff over many decades. Even on my first day, with a limited knowledge of anthropology, and while walking down the fifty-yard-long hallway, I notice differences amongst racially-associated features, differences that I was later able to associate with precise skull measurements, some quite subtle, some obvious, by the paleoanthropologists in the department. Carefully labelled categories show the two main Bantu-derived black tribes; the Nguni (further divided into Xhosa, Zulu, Ndebele and Swazi) and Sotho-Tswana. Their features are distinctly different from the Khoisan, made up of the Hottentots and the closely related Bushmen. Sparsely represented on the walls are death masks of Asian and Indonesian people, their scant presence reflecting the rarity of migratory patterns of those groups to South Africa. The 'Europeans' also seem to exhibit varying features, representing the heterogeneous origins of settlers from Holland, Germany, England, Scotland, Ireland and France, with a smattering from Mediterranean, Eastern and Northern European countries.

I breathe deeply, as I hold open the old wood and glass doors to the dissection hall and walk into the brightly lit hall with white walls which houses twenty-six cadavers covered with clean yellow plastic sheets, lying on marble-topped wooden tables. This is to be my laboratory of learning for twelve hours per week from early January through November 1962. For several years, I had imagined my first day at medical school, but nothing prepared me for the smell of cadavers embalmed in the formaldehyde-laced preserving fluid.

The silence is eerie, punctuated by the sounds of leather shoes on the tiled floor, the rustling of white coats brushing past the plastic covers and by the restrained, soft murmurings of a dozen or so men and women in immaculate starched white coats, our anatomy teachers, six of whom are recently graduated physicians called 'table docs,' taking a year out of their post graduate training to teach and learn anatomy, mainly to be better prepared for the South African and United Kingdom primary Fellowship examination in Surgery. They direct us to our assigned cadavers.

There are four students per cadaver. I greet the other three at my table. I'm assigned to pair with Patricia Nathan. Mike Eliastam and Basil Porter claim the left side of Archibald, a name we choose to call our male cadaver because it seems so unique, appropriate and unforgettable. The air is thick with expectancy, apprehension, and uneasiness because we are in the presence of so many dead bodies, each area separated from the next cadaver by a four-foot high vertical wooden partition attached to a narrow desk and each of us sitting on a four-legged stool.

One of the differences between humans and other animals is that we know we're going to die whereas domestic and wild animals do not. From an early age we're aware that we will experience the death of loved ones. This predictable reality shapes our lives and often brings us a sense of meaning. The bodies are motionless and covered and my first thought is: where are they? Had they suffered during their last illnesses? Did they wonder what happens when one dies? Do we go somewhere, or do we just disappear?

Many of my Medical School friends believe in an afterlife, but I do not. Unlike some of my Catholic and Anglican acquaintances, who had attended funerals of loved ones as far back as elementary school, and who believed in death as a way of becoming united with deceased family members, friends, loved ones and Jesus in heaven, my Jewish background taught me to fear death since the real reward is thought to be here on earth living a pious, joyful life. I had learned from the Hebrew Bible that God had established a covenant with the people of Israel that promised those who followed His commandments would be granted descendants, that they would flourish, and that they would be given the land of Israel. But there is no promise of eternal life. In Psalms and Isaiah, the place people would go after death was called Sheol, a term that refers to some underground domain, without reference to reward or punishment. It is perhaps an anemic copy of life on earth, a place one wants to avoid if possible.

I had experienced the death of my maternal grandfather when I was eleven years old as a painful loss, and, to reinforce how tragic this was, I had to stay home while the adults went to the cemetery. That evening I could attend the prayer meeting and I saw the men cutting parts of their suits with razor blades; my Rabbi told me that this practice was based on the actions of the patriarch, Jacob, who tore his clothes when he thought his son Joseph had died. Watching these sinister and depressing activities made me believe that death was the absolute end of us.

My parents wouldn't let me attend graveside funerals until I was sixteen, and even then, it seemed like a morbid, depressing affair with lots of wringing of hands, crying, singing mournful prayers, people looking pale and depressed, often wearing sunglasses to hide their tears, and the thud of soil on the coffin as people dumped fistfuls of dirt into the open grave.

I sat 'shiva' (Hebrew for 'seven' days) with my mother and grandmother on low sofas with cushions removed, curtains drawn, in dark rooms with heavy carpets and furniture, mirrors and pictures covered with sheets, and mournful prayers sung by bearded rabbis, cantors and other men in black suits and heavy black hats. My bereaved aunts and uncles seemed solemn and sad. It was very quiet in my grandma's home, in contrast to Mark Twain's description of a hilarious wake in 'Huckleberry Finn,' or stories by Irish friends who told of wakes overflowing with lots of booze, food, laughter and jokes. Humor seems to me an inappropriate accompaniment to death, but I certainly tolerate it in my non-Jewish friends since they seem to celebrate it as an inevitable opportunity to achieve eternal happiness.

The Anatomy department had risen to world prominence under the direction of Raymond Dart whose discovery of a new species of hominid, which he named *Australopithecus Africanus* in 1924, created heated arguments about the origins of Man. Dart was the subject of cynical antagonism for twenty-five years for daring to claim that Man originated in Africa, not in Europe as many European and North American scholars of the late nineteenth and early twentieth century believed. His contributions and hypotheses were only recognized and accepted in the nineteen fifties when his fame exploded worldwide.

In 1951 Dart appointed the recently graduated Philip Valentine Tobias to a full-time lectureship, equivalent to a modern-day Assistant Professor. The two of them became lifelong friends and colleagues, and together they greatly contributed to the development of modern paleoanthropology and the 'Cradle of Humankind in Africa,' formally created by the university in recognition of the enormous paradigmatic shift in beliefs as to where Man originated.

It is soon clear that my first day in the dissection hall is not an ordinary introduction to our medical school. Four clergymen stand on either side of Professor Tobias at the front of the large dissection hall. Rabbi Lapin from the Yeoville Orthodox synagogue, Anglican Bishop Stradling, Catholic Bishop Hugh Doyle, and Sheikh Abdul Basit 'Abd us-Samad of the Islamic community are there. This is to be a mass funeral to be conducted by men of faith.

The solemn ceremony is conducted by Tobias, at thirty-six the youngest Departmental Chairman in the entire medical school, a renowned paleoanthropologist and anatomist and already a legend in the corridors of academia. Despite his short stature, no more than five feet six inches, he is an imposing presence, his angular face dominated by an exuberant flourish of carefully managed black hair, and a large beak-like nose highlighted by a neatly trimmed black moustache.

He very quickly seems to tower over everyone because of his meticulously clean white coat and his commanding, distinct, clear, poised, dramatic, mellifluous voice, as striking and dramatic as a Shakespearian actor, as he welcomes us. His words are peppered with poetry and literary quotes, referring to the great traditions of previous generations of students who had passed through these magnificent halls, and with reminders that we are dealing with precious human material that should be treated with the utmost respect.

Professor Tobias starts the burial ceremony by telling us how fortunate we are to learn from the dead. They have donated their bodies to science for us to glean wisdom and become competent practitioners of the art and science of medicine, dentistry, physical therapy and occupational therapy. Throughout the coming academic year, we should remember that these are human beings, and we need to treat them with respect and dignity. We will spend at least twelve hours a week dissecting their tissues, unraveling the marvels of human anatomy. We must remember to behave with all the dignity and gratefulness that we can muster. Today we honor their contribution with a multi-denominational funeral representing Jews, Christians and Islamic people. This solemn occasion will remind us how privileged we are to be in the presence of anatomic perfection created by the Almighty.

He describes the embalming process, how each cadaver is injected with an embalming solution after death. Each body is bagged in a watertight and airtight container and placed separately in stainless steel cabinets, each on its own shelf that can be drawn out on casters. The cadavers in the dissection halls stay on the sturdy wooden tables for eleven months while we dissect them, dousing them every day with fresh solutions of the preservative, prepared by the anatomy staff. He also talks about some of the legal and ethical aspects of cadaver accrual and maintenance.

The presence of religious leaders is not an accident. I am struck by the similar ideas and presentations of Professor Tobias and the four clergy. We are all human beings in a large universe and we need to respect each other, in life and in death. Tobias reminds us of a depiction on a sarcophagus in a Massachio fresco in the Santa Maria Novello Church in Florence, Italy, which when translated from the Italian reads: 'I once was what you are and what I am you will also be.' It is indeed a stark reminder of both the inevitability of death and how we should respect our cadavers as we do ourselves.

Each of the faiths is represented by both a ritual prayer and a short sermon on the sacred meaning of our privileged experience of precious human beings who had been just like us, alive, breathing, moving, working, thinking, and with friends and families. Many of the deceased had donated their bodies to science with the specific understanding that they would be contributing to furthering the knowledge of students who would someday use that knowledge to help patients with illnesses.

We will not know our cadavers by their real names. Tobias urges us to imagine how cherished every one of them was to their families and friends. We are to be the caretakers of these treasured people and, depending on the wishes of their loved ones, their carcasses will eventually be returned to the families for burial or cremation.

I feel enormously fortunate and uplifted by the rich ceremony that honors the dead. I will respect these dead people as if they are my own family.

I no longer feel uncertain about the cadaver I'm about to meet. In retrospect that ceremony made me feel reverence for the living and the dead, unleashing a powerful compassion for the magnificence of the human body, giving me a confidence in what I was to become, fearing death less and open to the challenge of saving lives.

Instead of fainting, I am inspired, and anxious to remove the plastic cover, and to meet my cadaver. We start dissection in earnest the next day. It is time to meet our cadaver. I hold my breath. This would be my first glimpse of a dead person. Pat, Mike, Basil and I take the yellow plastic sheet off the cadaver.

Chapter Fifteen:

༄

A Special Beach

Marianne and I chat regularly on the telephone and by letter, postcard and, as the internet era matures, by email. We discuss her health, new doctors, and her job as a speech therapist in the Los Angeles school district. She is doing very well, although she still has pain in her neck and spine. The memories of severe pain and suffering she had endured from her massive surgeries, chemotherapy, and radiation treatments, still haunt her. She doesn't complain or seek sympathy. She reveals how grateful she feels *for* the discomfort.

Emotional and spiritual growth had followed from the exhaustive medical treatments and her flourishing transcendent life. Initially, I don't understand how anyone could be grateful for suffering. But I cannot ignore the significantly favorable effects of Marianne's affliction on her mindset. I hear similar thoughts from patients whose treatment regimens are quite difficult.

My own experience of non-ordinary states of consciousness through Holotropic Breathwork is essential for my understanding of how suffering might enhance spiritual awareness and healing. Recalling a bout of hepatitis, I had when I was in the second grade, remembering how weak and nauseated I had felt, and sensing from my mother's fear that I might not survive, I began to understand Stanislav Grof's many ideas on the striving for self-awareness and the focus on transpersonal approaches to human behavior.

While searching primitive cultures for methods that could consistently induce a state of spiritual ecstasy, Grof became fascinated with Shamanism. The primitive rituals used by shamans have a lot to teach modern physicians about pain, suffering, empathy, and the spiritual dimension of healing. During my medical school and residency training in South Africa, I occasionally met witch doctors and saw the trust placed in their healing abilities by rural, tribal, and even city-dwelling Africans. Shamans would sometimes experience 'symbolic death and annihilation at the hands of the spirits' as a way of experiencing the darkness of the human condition by actually facing extreme physical and emotional illness themselves. A tribal man or woman striving to become a fledgling shaman would have to leave the mundane physical world and experience a journey to the otherworld of the spirits involving a near-death state, recovery, and rebirth. The newly initiated shaman would come to understand suffering and be reborn as a person of compassion and healing with the understanding that we are all connected and where one suffers, so we all do. Shamanism allows us to draw upon our own personal experience of pain. If we're able to leave our individuality behind, we might journey into the 'otherworld' to find a cure for our patients.

Like many physicians in training, I had read a modern edit of the Hippocratic Oath during the graduation ceremony from medical school. I vividly thought about one phrase I recited at my medical school graduation, in a modified form, that related to compassion that is so valued amongst healers: 'In whatsoever house I enter, there will I go only for the benefit of the sick.' The great 12th-century Jewish physician and sage, Maimonides, said it as well: 'May I never see in the patient anything but a fellow creature in pain.' Somehow, my personal Holotropic Breathwork experience – what I recall as my journey through a lighted tunnel of experiencing an entire lifetime of conscious and unconscious memories in a short time period – enabled me to extend my understanding of suffering and illness in a very deep way.

Marianne and I continue to talk by telephone and, occasionally, exchange postcards and letters. We share accumulating memories about our lives. Constantly seeking a committed relationship, she talks about every new romantic interest. The stories are always quite similar. She meets a handsome young man who sweeps her off her feet, and she calls or writes me to tell me about him. She is hopeful that this is 'the one.' She so wants to be married and to have children. I listen and mirror her excitement. The joy is often tempered by a painful rejection when the suitor discovers her past cancer diagnosis and treatment.

She meets Gary fourteen years after her surgeries when she is thirty-seven. He is forty-nine, divorced, has three teenage children, and manages a book publishing company. Unlike the other men, he does not walk away when he discovers her medical past.

She takes him to Esalen for a weekend.

'He loved being there,' she tells me. 'I took him across the creek to the Big House and down the steps to the little beach. You know the one I mean. That's the beach you and I like so much.'

Water flows through a gorge in the steep mountains, bisecting the Esalen property, the Big House built by Michael Murphy's grandfather on the north slope, and into the Pacific Ocean, creating eddies, tide pools with an abundance of small sea creatures including crabs, abalone, mussels, sea anemones, and starfish that provide food for the birds and larger creatures. I can stand still and listen to the gentle waves caressing the rocky beach in a small alcove and feel a soft breeze wafting eastward from the sea. Occasionally, I see seagulls and seals basking in the sun and, once, a humpback whale about three hundred yards out in the ocean. Marianne and I often share memories of the sunset seen from that tranquil spot, which I visit repeatedly over the years. I call her from Esalen every time I go there. It is our own special place, a place for us to share and reminisce about her miraculous 'cure' that we both treasure and celebrate.

Marianne is excited when she reveals that she and Gary will be married in the spring of 1994. She writes me the details of her dress, the layout of the church, the reception, and the catering. I rejoice at the pictures of her in a wedding dress standing proudly beside the groom.

I hear from her less often after her wedding, but I feel her presence whenever I see new cancer patients. I remember Marianne's gentle reminder: 'Your patients are scared. They look to you to provide hope. Speak to them as if they are your best friends. Find a way to encourage them and accept whatever they feel will be best for them.'

When I receive Gary's letter, delivered by express mail eleven years later, I am apprehensive. Why would he send the letter by express mail? Why now?

'Dear Doctor,

Marianne's mom and I talked about you this morning. We're all in a state of shock. She was only forty-nine. I came home from work a few nights ago and found her unconscious in the bathroom. The ambulance came and took her to the local hospital, and they said she had bled into her gut but would be alright. They kept her in the intensive care unit and gave her blood transfusions. I stayed for a while and then went home. They called me early the next morning and told me to come quickly. When I got there, she was gone.

I want you to know she often talked about you. You helped her in many ways. I'd love to meet you sometime. Please let me know when you're in Southern California again.

Gary'

An internal earthquake has struck me, and I excuse myself and find an empty clinic room, close the door and sit down, staring out the window at the Midtown skyline. I feel like an African python has encircled me and is rapidly squeezing me, my breath labored against the immense force, terrified by the feeling of imminent suffocation, a deep pain emerging from my abdomen, and images of Marianne playing in my mind. I see her curled up on the examining table with a giant, protuberant abdomen. I see her waiting for surgery, her head bald after chemotherapy, looking so lonely, tiny, emaciated and scared on the gurney. I see her under anesthetic in the UCLA Medical Center OR, and the massive operation, remembering her massive tumor as we removed it from her abdomen. I see her as a beautiful thirty-three-year-old in a restaurant in Santa Monica and I remember her lovely smile. My friendship with her has changed me so much and my attitudes towards patients and trainees has matured to the point that I'm able to comfortably interact with everyone as a caring physician.

My mind races around the information surrounding her death. Blaisdell's words to the residents in the UC Davis Surgical Training program reverberate with me: 'No one should die of hemorrhage.'

What did the physicians in Camarillo do, or fail to do, with Marianne? I'm blaming them for her death. Then I realize that she probably had an incurable complication of prior radiation to her small intestine which led to bleeding that perhaps could not have been amenable to even the most expert surgical intervention.

'Dear Gary,

Your card and the newspaper obituaries were unexpected and sobering. Thank you, also, for sharing excerpts of her 1994 diaries.

My first reaction to Marianne's death was utter disbelief and deep sadness.

She has lived so vividly in my mind for 26 years that I could not imagine her gone. But, she is still with me, as she always was, in my soul.

She transformed me when I was a relatively young surgical oncologist in training at UCLA. She introduced me to the Esalen Institute in Big Sur and I learned why she herself had been transformed, at age 23, by her first visit to that magical place of awareness and consciousness. She traveled there often in the first few years after her heroic surgeries, chemotherapy and radiation therapy in late 1979 and early 1980. She explored the precious moments of her survival with courage and quiet determination and she lived bravely with pain. I don't think she was ever without pain of some sort, but she never complained.

We remained in contact after I moved to Michigan and she shared many private thoughts with me. I learned a lot from those thoughts. I learned that, while I could accomplish many technological, often magical, skills, gleaned from my training, that they lacked true human interaction that became possible for me because of Marianne's wisdom. She taught me to look deeply into the souls of my patients. She stopped fearing death, believing it could be calm and tranquil and that has allowed me to be more accepting of my own death, and to face patient deaths without feeling a sense of failure.

I realized that all the dogmas from my medical school and surgical teachers were lacking the importance of the deep interpersonal attachment that is possible between a doctor and a trusting patient. My interactions with all my patients since that time have become richly endowed with a greater understanding of patients' humanity.

We are all patients at one time or another, vulnerable to pain, suffering, tragedy and death. We all have family and friends who worry about our welfare. We all deserve the best scientifically-based treatments, and the compassion and honesty of caring physicians who recognize their own vulnerability.

I vividly remember meeting Marianne at a restaurant in Santa Monica when I returned to the Southland for a visit. I had not seen her for a few years and she looked glorious. Whenever I think about her I remember that beautiful sight.

I can't help thinking about Marianne's mother and the rest of her family. Please pass on to the them my heartfelt condolences for their loss.

I hope we can meet one day.

David Nathanson'

The death of a patient is often viewed as an admission of failure by many physicians. Perhaps we made an error or chose a treatment option that other doctors would not have chosen. I thought about how I would have managed her bleed. Maybe the community hospital should have transferred her urgently to a large academic center with skilled interventional radiologists to do the common procedure of vessel embolization where a small wire coil or a ball of a cotton-like material is inserted into the leaking artery through a catheter. I'm no longer convinced that a more aggressive approach would have stopped the bleeding. She had received radiation to parts of her intestine that might have caused long-term changes that increased the risk of bleeding. I am so sad, frustrated and disappointed, and at first, I don't focus on the positive that she had lived twenty-six years after treatment of a potentially lethal cancer. I just want her to be alive and to be present for her friends, family and me.

Ernest Becker's basic premise in his 1973 Pulitzer prize-winning book, *Denial of Death*, is that human civilization is ultimately an elaborate, symbolic defense mechanism against the knowledge of death. Many of us develop an emotional and intellectual response to knowing of our own mortality by denying it in some way. We know the reality of material death, and we try to transcend that mindset by symbolically evading the obvious physical demise in our minds by creating something that will last forever, something that will never die - like faith in a Higher Power.

I wrestle with Marianne's death and feel forlorn, but I eventually understand that the part of her that lasts forever is her courageous presence in my memory. By initially beating the incredible odds and surviving for twenty-six years, she taught me to accept my own death, a process that I had never incorporated into my soul, even though I was exposed to corpses in medical school and, later, the deaths of patients in my clinical practice.

Before my transformative experience at Esalen in 1990, I, like many of my physician colleagues, felt uncomfortable talking to patients who were dying. It was even more difficult for me to talk to family members when I knew there was no further medical treatment that would save the lives of their loved ones. When questioned by the family or the patient, I responded with terms that were designed to ease the pain of realization. While soothing over the harshness of the real prognosis, I was also myself convinced 'it was not so bad.' Marianne's candor and her demand for absolute honesty encourage me to feel comfortable with patients, to look them in the eye and to talk frankly about the cancer diagnosis and prognosis.

If we face life with courage, hope, and gratitude – especially in the face of intense suffering – we will cope.

Gary had a dilemma. Marianne's family wanted her buried in a cemetery close to their homes in Los Angeles. But he knew where she would want her final resting place. He struggled with the conflict for a few weeks and then drove up north from Los Angeles to Big Sur, the urn with her ashes carefully secured on the floor on the passenger side of his car. The security officer at the front gate at Esalen, after receiving approval from the administration, allowed him onto the property.

He parked his car near the Big House and carried the urn down the steps to the beach below. Looking out towards the Pacific Ocean, then, gazing up towards the blue sky, he opened the urn and whispered a few words while emptying her ashes into the water at his feet. Now he and I can still talk to her. We can find her special beach, or we can talk to her in our hearts. It is there that she lives forever. It is there where all our loved ones live forever.

EPILOGUE

☙❦❧

This book describes how my initial education oriented me towards becoming manly and how surgical training made me arrogant and ruthless. My journey is a tale of my surgical training and practice and how I overcame the behavioral issues that many surgeons inevitably exhibit that leads to high rates of burnout, alcohol abuse, suicidal ideation and depression.

It is fifty-four years since I graduated from medical school and, unlike many surgeons my age, I continue to love being with patients. I've lived with surgeons for five decades and with the ancillary staff, such as nurses, anesthesiologists, scrub technicians, operating room janitors, surgical administrators. Most people identify surgeons as aggressive, over confident, egotistical and perhaps even unapproachable at a human level.

We surgeons are chosen by a rigorous process of 'weeding out' to train in this demanding profession based upon our intelligence, professionalism, conscientiousness, creativity, courage, and perseverance. We seem to fit the Introverted-Intuitive-Thinking-Judging Myers-Briggs test (INTJ) types with strong problem-solving, logical and organizational tendencies. We are often seen by others as confident, dependable, structured, hands-on, industrious, and meticulous; but also, as being **angry**, irritable, impatient, argumentative, belligerent, domineering, arrogant, hostile, impersonal, egocentric, and poor communicators.

A good surgeon, one who consistently attains the accolades of patients and their families, favorable recognition by colleagues, outstanding peer-review by professional organizations (such as Press-Ganey), and the reliability of good outcomes from surgical procedures, must exhibit superior manual dexterity and three-dimensional imagination. A surgeon must certainly know how to do an operation perfectly. He/she must also know when to operate on a diseased organ and, perhaps more difficult, when not to operate. But it is not enough to be competent in accomplishing the physical side of a surgical procedure. We must also be good clinicians, able to diagnose difficult diseases and to manage complications that occur during and after surgical procedures. We must also manage ethical, moral, cultural, and financial issues associated with our surgeries.

I wanted to be a great surgeon and I knew I had to be dedicated, willing to sacrifice my time to patients, even when it meant missing dinner, or a long-planned party with family, or my son's fencing try-outs, or my daughter's middle school graduation. I had to persevere, even when a complication occurred in the middle of a procedure that prolonged the case from a planned four hours to an unexpected ten hours. During that time, I was responsible for the well-being of the patient. I learned how to change direction when something unexpected was found. I had to be decisive, and my decisions had to be accurate, precise and effective. I learned to be strong and sure-footed, and to lead teams of people in every operation. It's not surprising that I developed a large ego.

My surgical training, first in South Africa, then in North America, with some input from stop-overs in England and Scotland, gave me an enormous ego with a typical surgical personality.

Many of my surgical teachers had worked as surgeons during the second world war and, when they retired from the armed forces, and came to civilian practice, they brought with them the mindset of military medicine. They treated us with the discipline that they used in the army, air force or navy. The hierarchy was heavy with commands, judgements, threats and personally derogatory behavior. I coped as best I could, often by smoking cigarettes, drinking alcohol, and indulging in frenetic sports activities, and raucous parties. I could not discuss the stresses of surgical training with anyone and I didn't know how to process my stress. My fellow trainees talked about our patients, but we didn't admit to any mistakes that resulted in horrendous complications and death. Instead we 'manned up,' saying nothing about our feelings or emotions, stuffing our caring selves deep inside, not letting anyone know that we had any problems.

I developed a surgical personality. Surgical training after medical school was brutal and proved to be a depersonalizing experience. A mixture of harsh and personally derogatory teachers and lack of sleep made me ruthless. I wanted to be just like my teachers because they seemed so perfect. I treated younger trainees under me with the same harshness that I had been treated.

What is a surgical personality? I had learned how to be a surgeon in every sense, often feared by medical students, surgical residents and nurses, using a sharp tongue and an arrogant demeanor to make sure that everything around me functioned like a well-oiled machine.

I learned to exhibit superb clinical and operating room skills and became an ego-filled, militaristic, narcissistic, manly man, who had lost his innate caring and humanity, an awareness of which I only realized after I befriended Marianne, the young woman patient described in this memoir who was dying of a massive abdominal tumor. I worked with my chief at UCLA, the world-renowned surgical oncologist, Donald Morton, on her case. I thought I and the team that worked with me had given her a little longer to live, but, while acknowledging our input, she had a different idea about why she had survived and flourished for a further twenty-six years after her surgery. She told me that her visits to the Esalen Institute in Big Sur, California, had given her the courage to conquer her tumor. She had come to terms with the possibility of dying, only to find that she was determined to live.

When I explored the Esalen Institute, I came to understand that her determination probably played a major part in her healing and I visited the place to find out more about healing practices that I had not previously encountered. My discovery of the mind-body connection while doing a workshop at Esalen propelled me into an almost mystical state of mind and turned my behavior back to what I had been as a child and adolescent. I became more of what I had been in my youth – kind, thoughtful, caring, empathetic and altruistic.

My 'rebirth' experience left me relieved, happy, humble and content, but I worried that I would not be able to function as a surgeon as well as I had during my egotistical days. During surgical training in South Africa and in California I had been persuaded to believe that a competent surgeon had to be arrogant, nasty, overwhelming, overbearing, demanding, narcissistic and egotistical. How would I function if I now recognized my ego and wanted to live without it? Is it possible to be humble and yet effective as a surgeon in the operating room? 'Humility' may seem an unlikely way to describe a 'real' surgeon.

I felt that I had evolved as a human being when I awoke to my inner emotional self, but I thought I would not be as effective as a surgeon/scientist. I needn't have worried about my competence. My patients trusted me more because they saw my humanity. They cared about me as much as I cared about them. They asked me about my grandchildren and I proudly whipped out my cell phone to show them cute pictures. I can do this without feeling too vulnerable, a stark change from the way I was before my transformation. In the 'old days' I would have been cold and distant, and they would not have thought of me as someone with grandchildren. They would not have shared their own fears and vulnerabilities. They would not have trusted me to care for them as much as they do now.

Despite my rediscovered 'humanity,' and perhaps because of it, I have continued to treat cancer patients with ever-increasing skills and high-quality, enough to convince my patients, my hospital colleagues, medical students, surgical residents in training, university academic promotions committees, and City, State, National and International organizations that evaluate the abilities of surgeons, that I am amongst the top one percent of surgeons and cancer experts in the USA.

My experiences with other patients also educated and changed me. I changed because of Marianne, a dying patient who unknowingly exposed me to myself, in ways that were both unexpected and vitally important. If I had not had my transformative experience at the Esalen Institute in Big Sur, initiated because of her experiences there, I would not have looked inward and I would probably not have discovered that my patients share with me the divine within them.

When I truly recognized the beauty of another person, not only in their anatomy, pathology and physiology, but also in their wondrous souls, I came to realize that the entire healing relationship is founded upon friendship and trust. I discovered how to respond to the fear, worry and struggle of my patients by envisioning what it must be like to be them. Modern medical training has begun to embrace this idea by encouraging physicians to practice Mindfulness, an idea that would have been radical and crazy when I was a young surgeon.

Friendship with patients would have been impossible if I had continued to practice the way I was taught. After all, we usually reserve the term 'friend' to a small number of people in our lives with whom we share intimate trust. But I discovered another meaning for my friendship with patients. Without even knowing exactly how and why I was doing it, I found that I began to concentrate on deeply understanding my patients' feelings and emotions. I became willing to be open and to assume my place in an ongoing relationship based on trust, and a distinct need to know details of my patients' lives, details that obviously also required me to understand and embed myself in their medical conditions.

Other details became important for me and for my patients. I realized that I need to be equal to them, not superior, showing my willingness to relate openly and directly with them and their daily lives. My patients need to feel that I'm loyal, that they can rely on me to be there for them in times of joy and crisis as well. They need to feel my presence in the healing relationship as a non-judging, generous, caring, compassionate, hospitable person who is also their physician.

Initially, in my early years of training, my clinical notes were objective, and as dark and cold as a midwinter Michigan morning. There was nothing emotional and with no exposure of my own feelings. I did not record anything too personal about the patient. That changed after my own Marianne-induced midlife transformation. As I listened more carefully to the 'personal and friendly' parts of the patient's history, I asked and recorded personal details.

Patients often talk about their disrupted plans. They had planned a cruise, or had been excitedly looking forward to the birth of a grandchild, or the graduation of a daughter from college. They didn't expect the illness that now interferes with their plans. I recorded that in the clinical notes and, when I saw them months or years later, I had only to read my notes and to ask them follow up questions. That's what I do with my children when I remember important events in their own lives. I do that with friends. They know I care about them when I do that. I'm a reliable friend.

When patients realize that I care about them, when I go the extra mile to help them, they feel grateful. Gratefulness is a big part of our lives. Just thinking about 'Thanksgiving' is enough to clarify how important those words are. We celebrate the holiday once a year by inviting family and friends over for a ritual meal. I discovered that gratefulness is an attitude that makes me happy every day. I'm fortunate to have met Br David Steindl-Rast, whose authentic ideas on gratefulness, initiated though his theological, philosophical, literary, intellectual and spiritual explorations, together with his own personal experiences, have positively influenced many people.

I have made an unexpected but conscious effort to abandon the reptilian 'me-first' mentality that I had learned during my surgical career, finding comfort in those parts of me that were already there as a child and young adult, leaving space for the gratefulness and caring that have become my mantra. I had learned the Torah and the Talmud, sacred biblical and post-biblical texts, where I came to believe in the Divine Presence. That had elevated me to believe in all creatures, emptying me of egotism, resulting in a sense of freedom.

Imagine how strange it must have been to come face to face with an ideology which completely opposed my pious childhood origins. The ideology appeared in the form of teachers who espoused the development of manliness and toughness, first in elementary, then in high school, then in surgical residency and my early years in surgical practice. The mixture of kindness, compassion, empathy and healing, in stark contrast to the ruthless decisiveness that I practiced in my surgical career, would not have been possible until I 'woke up' to my new way of being following my Esalen transformation. Parts of me that lay dormant were re-activated.

I'm sure that it is easier to wall oneself from the suffering of others by ignoring personal feelings and emotions that are stirred by daily observance of major illness, especially the type that surgical oncologists like me see every day. How can one process the agonizing tears of a young spouse whose wife has just died from metastatic breast cancer? Watching the young children, bewildered by the loss of their mother and, perhaps, seeing their father cry, I had become used to moving away from this disturbing sight by setting my views on my next patient, a new challenge in the operating room. I didn't feel obliged to share in the grief. But my new self became unabashedly involved in mourning the death with the family, offering a hug, or a light shoulder touch, and a few comforting words. Instead of hiding away from distress, I moved towards the suffering. I felt the tragedy in my soul and the feeling was not accompanied by embarrassment, even when I, too, cried.

I became a surgeon who attracts complex cases, sometimes from a geo-graphic distance, partly because word of mouth travels far and wide. Surgical, clinical and scientific competence is vitally important but tender caring and empathy that accompanies that competence is priceless. I'm grateful that I saw the light.

Through Marianne, a woman who almost died in her twenties, but who lived fully for almost three more decades because of modern medicine and alternative therapies and faith, I learned an imperative truth that was re-cently voiced by the Dalai Lama: Honest concern for others is the key factor in improving our day to day lives. I learned that I could be warm-hearted, and, when in that state of mind, there is no room in me for arrogance, anger, jealousy, or insecurity.

CPSIA information can be obtained
at www.ICGtesting.com
Printed in the USA
LVHW031339040520
654973LV00020B/1965